FOR COUNTRY

FOR COUNTRY

MY LITTLE BIT TWENTY-ONE
MONTHS OF SERVICE

DONALD G. BARTLING

To order additional copies of this book, contact:
Xlibris
1-888-795-4274
www.Xlibris.com
Orders@Xlibris.com
699530

CONTENTS

DEDICATION

In order to encourage a greater appreciation for the service people that have served and paid the price to preserve the freedoms that we as United States citizens enjoy, I will attempt to convey some of the emotions and the actions that these people have done for this Nation over the course of its history.

I especially have in mind the names of the men that I knew and worked with that have paid the Supreme Sacrifice. They all received the Purple Heart posthumously. In view of the price that they paid, my contribution was truly only a "LITTLE BIT".

PREFACE

A study of history shows us that a Nation is only as strong as the will of its citizens to fight for it. America has been tested many times over in its relatively short history. From the Revolutionary War on down to the present conflicts in the Middle East, the majority of the American citizens were willing to place their lives and futures in danger to preserve and build the future of this Nation.

Even when the requirements of the military required the use of conscription in order to meet the needs of the day, most citizens were willing to shoulder their responsibilities and deliver the results that were of benefit to all Americans. Many times they have assured a future for this Nation by rising to the occasion. This is especially true today as the burden is falling on an entirely "volunteer force".

Unfortunately, there is always a (usually loud) minority that feel that our American way of life does not need protecting. Though they are wrong, they do immeasurable damage to the efforts that are being put forth by their fellow citizens. A brief review of the first half of the twentieth century shows us that we had been down this road before. Several factors played into the fact that we had been confronted with "nation threatening" situations several times during that time period. The world had been confronted with POWER HUNGRY nations twice prior to the current time. Each time we found ourselves unprepared to face the problems when they presented themselves. Our intelligence was either lacking or inadequate, and our military forces were weak and unable to respond in a timely manner to the threats that confronted us. That the American people are a peace-loving people is commendable; but there are times when they also must face reality. That reality is sometimes—WAR. This Nation responded with everything that was necessary to bring those tumultuous times to a proper conclusion. In the process hundreds of thousands of American military people sacrificed their lives for the cause. It had now become apparent that this conflict was no different from the preceding threatening situations. The threat of Communism to the peace and prosperity of the world and our Nation was now very clear, and it required a proper response.

An attempt will be made in this book to enlighten anyone that will listen that there was a time when it did not matter to the troops what their Serial No prefix was (RA, US, NG, or ER); they were in this to finish the mission that was before them.

The Korean War was the first action in which the Military was used as a racially integrated force. The units in which I served were of mixed races and that did not cause any difficulty for me, either as a member or as a NCO. There were isolated instances of individual prejudices surfacing. These were handled on an individual basis through the Military Justice System. Time has proven that this process can be successful.

CHAPTER 1

Induction and Basic Training

Immediately, upon the announcement of the invasion of South Korea by the North Koreans on June 25, 1950, I felt that I should prepare myself to be a part of that struggle. The premonition was correct as by November I was called for a physical examination, which I passed, and on December 18, 1950 I received my orders to report for induction into the Armed Service on January 12, 1951.

The following documents explain the procedures that were used at this time.

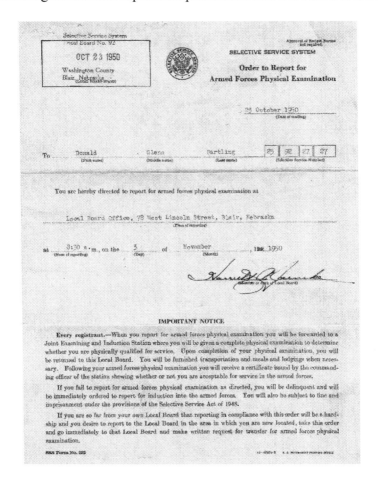

Mailed 6 Nov 1950

CERTIFICATE OF ACCEPTABILITY

LAST NAME - FIRST NAME - MIDDLE NAME	PRESENT HOME ADDRESS
BARTLING, Donald Glenn	Herman, Nebraska

SELECTIVE SERVICE NUMBER				LOCAL BOARD ADDRESS
25	92	27	27	Local Board #92 Washington County, Blair, Nebraska

I CERTIFY THAT THE QUALIFICATIONS OF THE ABOVE NAMED REGISTRANT HAVE BEEN CONSIDERED IN ACCORDANCE WITH THE CURRENT REGULATIONS GOVERNING ACCEPTANCE OF SELECTIVE SERVICE REGISTRANTS AND HE WAS THIS DATE:

[X] FOUND ACCEPTABLE FOR INDUCTION INTO THE ARMED SERVICES

[ ] FOUND NOT ACCEPTABLE FOR INDUCTION AT THE PRESENT TIME 1/

[ ] STATUS UNDETERMINED BECAUSE OF INCOMPLETE RECORDS

1/ Any inquiry relative to personal status should be referred to your Local Board

(DO NOT USE THIS SPACE)

DATE	PLACE	TYPED OR STAMPED NAME AND GRADE OF JOINT EXAMINING AND INDUCTION STATION COMMANDER	SIGNATURE
4 Nov 50	OMAHA, NEBRASKA	VARGE R. BUCK, 1ST LT., CE, USAR	*Varge R. Buck*

DD FORM NO 62
1 OCT 49

REPLACES NME FORM 62, 1 SEP 48, WHICH MAY BE USED.

SELECTIVE SERVICE SYSTEM

ORDER TO REPORT FOR INDUCTION

Selective Service System
Local Board No.

DEC 18 1950

Washington County
Blair, Nebraska

(LOCAL BOARD DATE STAMP WITH CODE)

18 December 1950

(Date of mailing)

The President of the United States,

To _____Harold_____ _____Glenn_____ _____Hartling_____ | 51 | 2 | 67 | 27 |
(First name)   (Middle name)   (Last name)   (Selective Service Number)

_____
(Street and number)

_____Herman_____ _____Nebraska_____
(City)   (State)

GREETING:

Having submitted yourself to a Local Board composed of your neighbors for the purpose of determining your availability for service in the armed forces of the United States, you are hereby ordered to

report to the Local Board named above at _____West Lincoln Street, Blair, Nebraska_____
(Place of reporting)

at __8:10__ A. m., on the _____17_____ day of _____January_____, 19_51_, for
(Hour of reporting)
forwarding to an induction station.

This Local Board will furnish transportation to the induction station where you will be examined, and, if accepted for service, you will then be inducted into a branch of the armed forces.

Persons reporting to the induction station in some instances are found to have developed disqualifying defects since being examined and may be rejected for these or other reasons. It is well to keep this in mind in arranging your affairs, to prevent any undue hardship if you are rejected at the induction station. If you are employed, you should advise your employer of this notice and of the possibility that you may not be accepted at the induction station. Your employer can then be prepared to replace you if you are accepted, or to continue your employment if you are rejected.

If you are not accepted, return transportation will be provided.

Willful failure to report promptly to this Local Board at the place specified above and at the hour and on the day named in this notice is a violation of the Selective Service Act of 1948, and subjects the violator to fine and imprisonment.

You must keep this form and bring it with you when you report to the Local Board. Bring with you sufficient clothing for 3 days.

If you are so far removed from your own Local Board that reporting in compliance with this Order will be a serious hardship and you desire to report to a Local Board in the area of which you are now located, go immediately to that Local Board and make written request for transfer of your delivery for induction, taking this Order with you.

You are advised to bring sufficient winter clothing - as it may be from three days to a week before your uniforms are issued.

_____[signature]_____
Member of Local Board.

SSS Form No. 252

U. S. GOVERNMENT PRINTING OFFICE 1948 O-783817

16—59801-1

Following the instructions that were sent in the Induction Notice, the group of Washington County inductees reported to the Selective Service Office in Blair at the specified time. They were then placed aboard a bus for the trip to Ft Omaha, in Omaha Nebraska. I, some of my friends, and others that were strangers to me were in that group.

Upon arrival at Ft Omaha we joined a much larger group of inductees from eastern Nebraska and western Iowa. Many new and long lasting friendships developed from this beginning of shared experiences that were ahead of the group members.

After a day of processing the men were told to line up facing the front of a large assembly room. We were sworn in as members of the U S Army by taking one step forward after the oath was read to us. This was a step into an unknown future, and was taken with many conflicting thoughts on the part of those that were participants of this event. Late in the day the inductees were transported by bus to the Union Station for an overnight rail trip to Kansas City. From Kansas City the train proceeded west to Ft.Riley, Kansas. The train arrived at Camp Funston, (a part of Ft Riley) late in the afternoon.

The next action was to pass through a warehouse where we were issued our uniforms and placed our civilian clothes in containers that were to be sent home for us; as trainees were not allowed to have civilian clothing during basic training. In speaking for myself—I felt a degree of pride in that uniform already at that point.

At this time and place we also received our military style haircuts. Since there were many styles going in, there was considerable change in the appearance of the group as a whole and some individuals in particular. The barbers were really being entertained by the reactions of some of the men that were rather vain about the hair-dos that were a source of pride to them. This action also became the first deduction from the "flying ten". This was an issue of $10 that was to be used for personal items that would be required in order to pass barracks inspections that were definitely in the near future. This was expected to be sufficient for those needs until the first payday which would be on the end of the month.

We were then transported to our training companies; mine and many of my friends turned out to be D Company, 87th Infantry Regiment, 10th Division. After receiving our barracks assignments, we were given our evening meal. We were then sent back to our barracks to receive more instructions from the Platoon Sergeant. My platoon Sergeant's name was Sgt. Hall.

At this time we were told that none of us would be leaving the company area for three weeks. We became well aware that there were orders and that they were to be carried out to the letter.

Lights were to go out at 10 o' clock and that time arrived with most of the new soldiers in their bunks. The certainty of that fact became very clear as "TAPS" was played at that time and the lights went out.
Early the next morning we hear the "wake up" call and everyone is expected to get out of their bunks immediately. Some are reluctant to accept the fact that from this time forward the call means exactly what it says. "Get Up Now": It was quite apparent that the ability to rise and shine early in the morning was much easier for the "farm boys" than for the "college" kids.

In a short time we were called out for "formation". "Roll call" was taken and we were sent to the "mess hall" for breakfast. The rest of the day was spent under the control of the training cadre—and they kept everyone busy. We were informed that we were to read the bulletin board every day to keep posted as to what was expected of each of the men. There was the "duty roster". There was a roster for "kitchen police" (KP), "guard duty", and garbage detail. I found early on that having a name that began at the beginning of the alphabet had a disadvantage; anyone in that position faced the almost certain possibility of getting an extra turn at all of the duties. This was true for me also, although I was not the only one that had to experience an extra KP, and guard duty.

It was apparent early on that there was a monstrous amount of learning that we needed to do in a relatively short time. Acceptance of that premise made the actual learning process much more palatable. Also this was going to be learning in areas in which most of the troops had no previous experience.

Instruction was given in all of the following areas:

1. Learn to take and follow orders and respect for authority.
2. Review the requirements of citizenship, and the responsibilities that must be accepted by the holders of that citizenship.
3. Develop a personal conduct that is cognizant of the persons that are around you, the public, and the foreign people, (if and when we come in contact with them).
4. Learn about and the use of the infantry weapons—M1 Rifle, M1 & M2 Carbine, Browning Automatic Rifle (BAR), light 30 Cal Machine Gun, 60 & 81 MM Mortars, Recoilless Rifle, 3.5 Bazooka, Grenades, 45 Cal Pistol, and 45 Cal Grease Gun.

Everyone received their dog tags. Information on them was name, serial number, blood type, and religious preference.

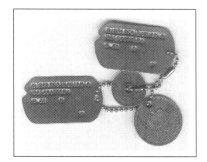

Rifle Inspection. Donald Bartling far right.

The most difficult part of the transition from civilian to military for most of the recruits was the loss of personal freedom to choose "what" and "when" a person could do anything. Total control of the activities and time had passed to the persons in authority.

In spite of that change, most of the guys were tired enough after each day that they went to sleep and in that manner accepted the new status.

Donald Bartling

L to R; First two unknown, John Luther, Lyle Wolf, Donald Bartling

The activities of each day included: 1.Dismounted drill; 2. Instruction in Military Conduct, 3. Weapons Instruction in nomenclature, care, and use. 4. Instruction in how to live in the outdoors, while maintaining health and effectiveness. As the days went by, it became apparent that the training was changing the men in many ways. They began to work as a team and to show a concern for each other. (I was to learn later that this ability to work in this fashion is of prime importance in having an effective military unit). It also began to show that a group of "people" will reflect the abilities and qualities of their leaders. Strong and fair leaders will earn the cooperation and respect of the sub-ordinate members. The end result is that these units will be able to accomplish many results that are beyond expectations.

January and February of 1951 turned out to be warmer and drier than normal for this part of Kansas. This made the outdoor activities much easier to accomplish. However, this was not to continue for the entire period. In March the Company went on its first bivouac. We marched out to the bivouac area in quite warm and dry weather; but this was about to change. We pitched our 2-man pup tents and prepared for the night. We had been well instructed as to how to pitch the tent and prepare the drainage around it, but as is usually the case, not everyone carried out the instructions carefully enough. In the middle of the night a thunderstorm came up and it made the tents that were not properly drained very uncomfortable. I and my tent mate Leo did not have the problem as we had picked a well drained spot to place our tent. We also trenched around it in the proper manner. We were dry and comfortable throughout the 6-day bivouac. The next day we had about 8-10 inches of snow to contend with; we had no problem with that either. This was also our first exposure to the "field kitchen". Eating our meals in the dark and cold was not an activity that most enjoyed, but we adjusted to the discomfort in a relatively short time. The desire for a full stomach out-weighed the desire to "skip-it".

Due to the fact that we were being trained as infantry, the emphasis was on our being efficient with the infantry weapons. Our main weapon was the MI rifle. We had to

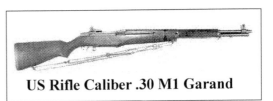

US Rifle Caliber .30 M1 Garand

be able to break it down, clean, and reassemble it by touch. At first, that seemed difficult, but we soon learned that we could do it. Everyone bad

Grenade Throwing

to qualify on the "firing range" with the M1. I managed to qualify as a Marksman; there were a number that qualified as Expert. Next we had to be familiar with the 30 cal carbine. I also qualified as a Marksman with that weapon. We had familiarization firing of the 60 MM Mortar, the 30 cal air-cooled machine gun, the 57 MM Recoilless Rifle and the 2.36 inch Bazooka. Familiarization was also required for the Grenades. It was very obvious at the start that the use of "duds" was a necessary precaution as the art of throwing the grenades requires some practice.

During the remaining weeks of basic training we were exposed to a number of "field problems". The first was known as "General Bells Problem". In this we were to attack and take a hill with the use of live ammunition. There was also covering mortar fire, this required that orders be carried out precisely and carefully. If the force moved too quickly it could be exposed to the mortar fire, and if you moved too slowly you had better plan to do it again. The second field problem was "infiltration fire". It consisted of walking through the course with the rifles firing at pop-up targets. It was to resemble the environment of going into a town with cover for the enemy. One could use up a large quantity of ammunition in a very short time in this exercise. Toward the end of the training period we went on the second bivouac for another five or six days. The time was late April. The weather was pleasant until the last day; this was the day that we were to go through the "infiltration course" twice, once in the afternoon and again in the dark of night. This exercise was to teach us how to crawl on the ground under machine gun fire with explosive charges exploding around us as we advanced through the course. The afternoon exercise worked quite well, but the night problem was done in a wild thunderstorm. We were a very muddy and messy company of men when we started our march back to camp. The distance was about eight miles and took us about three hours of marching. After our arrival back at the barracks our first duty was to clean everything, the rifle was the first to get cleaned, as no one wanted to have any rust on his rifle at inspection time. There was not much time for sleep that night, but the time that we did have was very refreshing.

One building that worried many of the trainees was—the gas chamber. Every trainee knew that there was a date on which he would go through the gas chamber. That day arrived for our company too. It was a rather warm and muggy day in spring and the air was quiet and heavy. We were to learn how to use the gas masks. We went in with the masks on and then were told to remove them in the "tear gas" that was released in the building. Our eyes immediately began to burn and water as we were escorted from the building into the outside air. Relief was immediate, but not total, and the residual fumes aggravated us for some time after. It was especially noticeable as we went for our noon meal in the "mess hall". We had a second round of intense watering of the eyes as we ate our meal. We had learned well the need for the gas masks.

An important part of military training and life is—guard duty. It is a prime importance in times of war and in combat zones. I did not find it difficult to walk my post at night, but a person does think of the dangers that may be present in combat areas. We were required to learn and abide by the GENERAL ORDERS.

GENERAL ORDERS

1. TO TAKE CHARGE OF THIS POST AND ALL GOVERNMENT PROPERTY IN VIEW.
2. TO WALK MY POST IN A MILITARY MANNER, KEEPING ALWAYS ON ALERT.
3. TO REPORT ALL VIOLATIONS OF ORDERS I AM INSTUCTED TO ENFORCE.
4. TO REPEAT ALL CALLS FROM POSTS MORE DISTANT FROM THE GUARDHOUSE THAN MY OWN.
5. TO QUIT MY POST ONLY WHEN PROPERLY RELIEVED,
6. TO RECEIVE, OBEY, AND PASS ONTO THE SENTINAL WHO RELIEVES ME ALL ORDERS FROM THE COMMANDING OFFICER, OFFICER OF THE DAY, AND OFFICERS AND NON-COMMISSIONED OFFICERS OF THE GUARD ONLY. 7. TO TALK TO NO ONE EXCEPT ON THE LINE OF DUTY.
8. TO GIVE THE ALARM IN THE CASE OF FIRE OR DISORDER.
9. TO CALL THE CORPORAL OF THE GUARD IN THE CASE NOT COVERED BY INSTRUCTIONS.
10. TO SALUTE ALL OFFICERS AND ALL COLORS AND STANDARDS NOT CASED.
11. TO BE ESPECIALLY WATCHFUL AT NIGHT AND, DURING THE TIME FOR CHALLENGING, TO CHALLENGE ALL PERSONS ON OR NEAR MY POST AND TO ALLOW NO ONE TO PASS WITHOUT PROPER AUTHORITY.

During the last months of training we were often given weekend passes. In order to enjoy these passes, transportation became an important part of utilizing the time to the best advantage. Many of us went home if we could feel certain that we could return by check-in time. Automobiles were very helpful in order to accomplish these trips in a timely manner.

As trainees we were not allowed to have automobiles in the Camp area. We were fortunate in that the citizens of Ogden, Kansas, a small town just outside of the east entrance to Ft Riley would rent the trainees a spot to park their cars on their lots. Many had the front yards covered with automobiles most of the time. I was charged one dollar a week for the privilege of parking my car in one of those private yards. The use of the car gave us the opportunity to explore some of the surrounding country and towns on the weekends that we did not go home.

Our training was completed around the first of May. At this point we were a very sharp marching unit and showed up well in the parades. Then the emphasis shifted to where will each of us be assigned and how soon. In my company most of the trainees were placed in the pipeline and ordered to report to Ft Lawton Washington. They received a few days at home and then were to be assigned to the Far East Command (FE COM) when they reported in Ft Lawton. I fully expected to be in that group of soldiers, but the higher authorities had determined otherwise. I was assigned to the 25th Field Artillery Battalion in Camp Funston. At that time they were the entity that administered the Leaders Course for Ft Riley.

CHAPTER 2

Leader's Course

Upon reporting to the 25th Field Artillery Battalion we were introduced to our Team Leaders and Instructors. They welcomed us and gave us an orientation on what we could expect and also what was expected of the Candidates. We were informed that we would have no duties other than keeping ourselves, our cubicles, and the barracks clean and in good order. The rest of our time would be spent in class and study. We were told that their expectation of us was—that we do our best and that failure to complete the course would not be a "black mark" on our records.

We were then given this letter from General Moore:

HEADQUARTERS 10TH INFANTRY DIVISION
Fort Riley, Kansas

SUBJECT: Welcome to the Leaders Course

TO: Candidates of the Leaders Course

You have been selected as a potential leader. Your previous unit commander felt that you possess the latent qualities which are characteristic of a leader.

At no time in the history of our nation has the need for leadership been greater. Our mission – success in battle – can be achieved only through competent leadership.

The Leaders Course is designed to develop in you those qualities necessary for leadership. We will lay the foundation here; your success as a leader in the future will depend on how well you apply yourself to your work here, and how well you seize opportunities to practice good leadership throughout your career.

J. E. MOORE
Brigadier General, United States Army
Commanding

General Moore's Letter

THE LEADERS CODE

"I become an Army Leader by what I do. I know
my strength and my weaknesses, and I strive cons-
tantly for self improvement. I live by a moral code
with which I set an example that others can emulate.
I know my job and I carry out the spirit as well as
the letter of orders that I receive.

"I take the initiative and seek responsibility,
and I face any situation with boldness and confidence. I estimate the situation and make my own decision as to the best course of action. No matter
what the requirements, stay with it until the job is
done; no matter what the results, I assume full responsibility.

"I train my men as a team, and I lead them with
tact, with enthusiasm, and with justice. I command
their confidence and their loyalty; they know that
I would not consign to them any duty that I myself
would not perform. I see that they understand their
orders, and I follow through energetically to insure
that their duties are fully discharged. I keep my
men informed, and I make their welfare one of my
prime concerns.

"These things I do selflessly in fulfillment of
the obligations of leadership, and for the achieve-
ment of the group goal."

The Leaders Code

SUBJECT	TOTAL HOURS	PHASE I 1	2	3	4	PHASE II 5	6	7	8
a. Orientation Lecture	1	1	–	–	–	–	–	–	–
b. Final Instructions and graduation	1	–	–	–	–	–	–	–	1
c. Customs of the Service	1	1	–	–	–	–	–	–	–
d. Military Courtesy	1	1	–	–	–	–	–	–	–
e. Military Justice and Courts Martial	2	–	–	–	2	–	–	–	–
f. Physical Training	12	3	4	–	5	–	–	–	–
g. Dismounted Drill	14	3	5	–	6	–	–	–	–
h. Interior Guard Duty	3	–	–	–	3	–	–	–	–
i. Troop Information and Education	6	1	2	–	3	–	–	–	–
j. Inspection of Clothing and Equipment	4	2	1	1	–	–	–	–	–
k. Estimate of the Situation-elementary	2	2	–	–	–	–	–	–	–
l. Practical Work as Non Commissioned Officers and assistant Instructors with troops	183	–	–	–	–	49	49	49	36
m. Leadership (32 hours)									
(1) Introduction to Leadership	1	–	1	–	–	–	–	–	–
(2) Psychological Aspects	1	–	1	–	–	–	–	–	–
(3) Personal Adjustment	1	–	1	–	–	–	–	–	–
(4) Development of Personality	2	–	2	–	–	–	–	–	–
(5) Character of the Leader	1	–	1	–	–	–	–	–	–
(6) Round Table Discussion	1	–	1	–	–	–	–	–	–
(7) Roles of the Army Leader	2	–	2	–	–	–	–	–	–
(8) Objectives of the Leader	2	–	2	–	–	–	–	–	–
(9) Leader Subordinate Relations	2	–	2	–	–	–	–	–	–
(10) Round Table Discussion	1	–	1	–	–	–	–	–	–
(11) Solution of Leaders' Problems not involving Combat	2	–	2	–	–	–	–	–	–
(12) Combat Leadership	2	–	–	–	2	–	–	–	–
(13) Round Table Discussion	1	–	–	–	1	–	–	–	–
(14) Selection, Evaluation and Promotion of Army Leaders	1	–	–	–	1	–	–	–	–
(15) Leaders Reaction Test	12	–	–	12	–	–	–	–	–
n. Training Methods and Management (40 hours)									
(1) Military Training	2	2	–	–	–	–	–	–	–
(2) Principles of Learning	1	1	–	–	–	–	–	–	–
(3) Lecture Method	1	1	–	–	–	–	–	–	–
(4) Conference Method	1	1	–	–	–	–	–	–	–
(5) Demonstration Method	1	1	–	–	–	–	–	–	–
(6) Use of Reference Material	1	1	–	–	–	–	–	–	–
(7) Preparation & Use of Training aids	1	1	–	–	–	–	–	–	–
(8) Lesson Plan	3	3	–	–	–	–	–	–	–
(9) Class Management	1	1	–	–	–	–	–	–	–
(10) Methods of Testing	1	1	–	–	–	–	–	–	–
(11) Diction	4	4	–	–	–	–	–	–	–
(12) Application Stage	1	1	–	–	–	–	–	–	–
(13) Student Practical Application of Methods of Instruction	31	9	11	–	11	–	–	–	–

Master Program, page 1

	Hours								
o. Training of Small Units.................	4	-	4	-	-	-	-	-	
p. Small Job Management....................	4	-	-	4	-	-	-	-	
q. Methods of Instruction in Marksmanship (5 hours)(This subject is included in the student practical application in Methods of Instruction)									
r. Leading Small Units in Combat...........	31	-	3	28	-	-	-	-	
s. Leadership and Health..................	2	-	-	-	2	-	-	-	
t. Final General Class Critique...........	2	-	-	-	-	-	-	2	
u. Physical Conditioning.................	15	5	5	1	4	-	-	-	
v. Team Chiefs' Time.....................	11	3	-	3	3	-	-	2	
w. Movement to Phase II.................	4	-	-	-	4	-	-	-	
TOTAL HOURS	384	49	49	49	49	49	49	49	41

ANNEX 1 to TM No. 10, Hq, 25th FA Bn

Master Program, page 1

HEADQUARTERS
5421ST ASU RECEPTION CENTER
Camp Crowder, Missouri

Extracts from Armed Forces Talk 214

What is the Honor of a Serviceman?

Honor is a difficult thing to define. It means many things to many people. Almost everyone agrees that basically a man's honor is a series of values that he applies to his own behavior, as well as to the standards of his profession or calling.

An honorable serviceman must first be an honorable man and an honorable American. An honorable man distinguishes between right and wrong and attempts to do what is right. He keeps his promises. He wants to be proud of his actions. He recognizes the existence of a moral code and tries to live by it. No man is perfect, but an honorable man is ashamed of his faults and is not content unless he is striving to eliminate them and make his life more worthwhile.

An honorable American is a "good citizen". Citizenship imposes duties on every American. An honorable citizen cannot exercise his many rights and privileges as a citizen and at the same time, ignore his personal obligations to the country which makes these rights possible.

The personal and civic requirements of honor are applicable to every American, serviceman and civilian alike. In addition to these, however, the serviceman is bound by the military and naval codes of honor.

The honor of a serviceman has been traditionally considered particularly exacting. By reason of his oath, he assumes primary responsibility for the security of his country at all times, whatever the sacrifices or personal danger involved.

The basic requirement of the military code of honor is obedience to constituted authority - to the will of the American people as expressed through military leaders. Without loyalty to commanders and willing compliance with commands, the Armed Forces would become little more than a mob. In combat, a soldier who does not carry out orders can endanger the lives of many men. The penalties for disobedience, laid down in the Articles of War, indicate clearly that only cowardice and treason are more dishonorable.

Two other qualities distinguishing the honorable serviceman are truthfulness and honesty. Unless a serviceman can be relied upon for absolute honesty and truthfulness he cannot be relied upon at all.

In our enumeration of the principal qualities of a serviceman's honor we have left courage until last because it is difficult to conceive a serviceman without it. A serviceman without courage should be back home, he's in the wrong business.

Armed Forces Talk 214, page 1

Extracts from Armed Forces Talk 214 (What is the Honor of a Serviceman) Cont'd

The Nation's highest military decoration, bestowed for acts of supreme courage, is called the Medal of HONOR. Even among servicemen, however, there are misconceptions about courage that should be cleared up.

First of all, courage, by itself, is not necessarily admirable. A gangster or bank robber can be physically courageous; so can a subversive agent or the jailer of a concentration camp. But courage is honorable only when its motive and objective are honorable. If the motive is dishonorable, the act is devoid of honor too.

In the second place, foolhardiness is not courage. The man who takes unnecessary risks is neither brave or courageous -- he is stupid.

Moreover, courage does not mean lack of fear. A man does not display courage when he takes a serious risk without knowing that he is in danger -- and, for most men, to be aware of danger is to be scared to some degree. It is when a man knows the danger and goes on anyhow, perhaps in spite of shaking hands and pounding heart, that he is truly courageous.

Nor is courage shown only in combat. The execution of many dangerous peacetime assignments -- research; testing, "dry runs" -- require a great courage. And to act contrary to the will of the "gang", to say emphatic "no", when some shady but attractive "deal" is suggested -- these and many similar situations call for moral courage of the highest order -- courage of the type that every serviceman is sooner or later called upon to have as a matter of personal and professional honor.

Now a word about the outward demonstration of respect fort worth and service which we call rendering honor. The Armed Forces do not render official honor casually or lightly. Their customs and ceremonies of honor have much significance.

The traditions of military courtesy are based on the assumption that anyone who wears the uniform and has won advanced grade, rating, or rank has proved himself worthy of it and should receive due respect and honor.

When a member of the Armed Forces shows outstanding special aptitude, skill, or courage in the performance of duty, he may receive honor in the form of a ribbon, badge, or medal. Wearers of such decorations are entitled to appropriate respect and honor.

Armed Forces personnel are expected to show special respect and give special honor to the National colors, the National Anthem, the Constitution, and elected public officials. Similar honor is accorded to flags and dignitaries of friendly foreign countries.

Anyone who has developed a sense of values finds it easy to honor persons, causes, and institutions that merit it. The Armed Forces strengthen this natural tendency by providing organized and formal means of showing respect. Ceremonies accompany the raising and lowering of the National Colors. A medal winner or a visiting dignitary may be honored by a formal parade. Other formalities help the serviceman remember and practice his obligation to render honor as well as to deserve it.

Armed Forces Talk 214, page 1

HEADQUARTERS
5421ST ASU RECEPTION CENTER
Camp Crowder, Missouri

Extracts from Armed Forces Talk 231

What are the rewards of Service?

Like every other calling, military service has certain drawbacks.
Lack of privacy is presented as a major hardship of Service Life. As a
rule servicemen cannot establish themselves in a community. To many
servicemen this periodic interruption of home life is a major hardship.
Others enjoy a change of scene now and then and look forward to new
assignments in strange places. Related to the frequent moving from
place to place is the necessity of leaving old friends. There is
another side of this situation. In their travel from place to place,
servicemen frequently renew old friendships that began at some earlier
assignment.

Now let's look at the other side of the picture, to examine some
of the recognized advantages of a service career.

The private gets a base pay of $75 per month. The average civilian
gets $213 per month. But the civilian pays out for essentials 92¢ of
each dollar of pay while servicemen use only $27 of his pay for essen-
tials. As a result the civilian can save $17 of his $213, while the
serviceman can save $48 of his $75.

A serviceman gets 30 days paid vacation each year, as against a normal 2 weeks for civilians.

Servicemen's liberal retirement benefits do not cost him anything
during his active duty years. Most civilian retirement benefits are
deducted from pay during active years.

Base pay of servicemen is supplemental by longevity Pay, overseas
pay, dependency allowances, and other "extras" for certain hazardous
service assignments.

As in civilian life, individual ability and willingness to study
and improve our skills are the keys to advancement. Opportunities are
literally unlimited, because of the constant need of capable leaders,
no other profession offers greater chance for recognition and reward
of individual ability.

Money, possession and security contribute to happiness, but are
not the source of happiness, regardless of occupation. The non-material
rewards of service, vital to self-respect and contentment, are a sense
of comradship peculiar to military organizations, prestige of the military
calling, and a sense of personal usefulness to our country. The servicemen knows that his regular job consists of the kind of good citizenship
that civilians often seek to perform outside their regular jobs.

Armed Forces Talk 231

This Course required eight weeks to complete. The first four weeks were in the Company Area and consisted of an intense schedule of classes and application. We also needed to practice giving commands. One feature that I really liked about this area was that—Reveille was played on the area speaker system and from that time on until Taps military march music was played continuously. We were exempt from the lights-out time as most of us needed from eighteen to twenty hours each day to get everything done properly. The second four weeks usually required application of our knowledge in one of the training companies as part of the training cadre. We started our Class102 with over 100 candidates, at graduation time we had just over 60 remaining.

The environment in the Leaders School was very much different than in the Basic Training Co. The personal space was much larger than the "upper' and "lower" bunks that we had become accustomed to in basic training. There are two men per cubicle. I found my new cubicle partner to be a very friendly and pleasant person to be around; apparently he felt the same about me as we got along very well.

The day began early in the morning and we needed to work very late at night. The purpose of this was to test our ability to handle long hours and still be functional. The hours often were from 5 A. M. to 1 or 2 A.M. Some of the candidates could often be heard practicing dismounted drill commands as late as midnight down by the river, which was a short distance across the street from our company area.

The mess hall also was upscale from the basic training companies. There were tablecloths on the tables and the dining atmosphere was quite pleasant. Throughout the day there was music played from the company Orderly Room. Since I liked March music and the marches of John Philip Sousa. I liked that part of the atmosphere.

We were granted more privileges here than we had had in basic training. One that I really appreciated was that I could get a Post Permit that allowed me to bring my car on Post and park in the adjoining parking lot. I did not find much time to use it as we were busy almost all of the time except Sundays.

A national event took place while I was in the first phase of the Course. Over fifty cadets were dismissed from the West Point Military Academy for cheating on their tests. The result was that we were offered the opportunity to apply as replacements. I expected that there would be some that would want to take advantage of the opportunity, but by this time we had become determined to see this through and do our part in executing the Korean War. No one even asked about the opportunity. We all had friends that had gone on to Korea after completing basic training, and some had already become casualties. It seemed that most of the candidates felt that they did not want to "chicken" out, by taking advantage of this opening.

My place of duty for the Second Phase was C Co. 87th Infantry Regiment. This was just down the street from where I had been in D Company earlier in the year. This Company was just starting a new training cycle, so I could see how "green" I must have looked six months earlier. The first Sergeant, Sgt. Craig, was a very good manager of his duties. He was always aware of everything that needed attention, and working for and with him was a satisfying and learning experience. Since they were new and individuals like me had been hardened in physically it was easy to take them out for dismounted drill and calisthenics. After the first two weeks that ratio began to change as they developed the ability to endure more activity. I found that the instruction that I had received in the First Phase was valuable and when put to use could accomplish the purpose for which it was intended.

I found one event that was out of the ordinary during this phase. The Company had just finished the Infiltration Exercise when the Company commander realized that he had a problem. Under no circumstances was there to be any live ammunition in the company area on Post. The ammunition depot closed at five o'clock. It had become too late to get there before closing time to return the unused ammunition. His solution was to have the "cadre" use up the "ammo" on a demonstration on this problem. About ten of us were given 11 clips of 8 rounds each to go through the course while the troops watched. We borrowed rifles from the recruits and went through the exercise. We used up all of the ammo in about fifteen minutes.

There had been heavier than normal rainfall during the months of May and June here in the Midwest. The heaviest of the rains of the longest duration were in Kansas. The Kansas River was about 200 yards from the barracks where I had been at the 25th Field Artillery Battalion. The soldiers from the Post had been patrolling the dikes for several weeks when on the sixth of July, my Class102 graduated from the Course. We were again housed in our original barracks.

Prior to Graduation we had a series of evaluation sessions. We were to report to the Instructors our experiences of Phase II. The most intriguing question for most of the men (myself included) was—How has your life been changed since you have become a soldier? There were many and varied answers. Many referred to the loss of their ability to control the simple daily routines of their lives since this control had passed to a higher authority. My answer was essentially this—Prior to becoming a soldier my efforts and desires were constructive and productive of materials for human comfort, but now my efforts had become directed in the opposite direction. I had to accept the need for "destructive" action in many instances—even to the destruction of human life; but that was also "constructive" in that the purpose for it was the protection of our Country and the citizens of it.

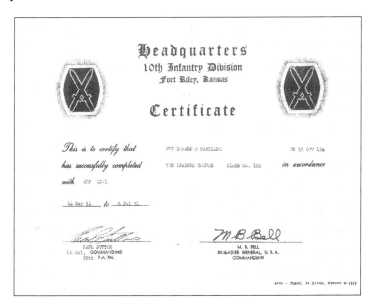

About a week was needed for us to process and leave for our next duty stations. We had not completed that when the flooding rivers became so high that though we had orders to leave, we could not do so as the roads were flooded. Everyone took their turns filling and carrying sandbags to build the dikes higher. It even came to the point that we used pillow cases and mattress covers as sandbags. The effort to save Camp Funston came to an end when the water came over the top of the sand-bags, and we were forced to pack up our field packs and head for the hills north of Highway 40. We formed up in "formation" and were marched past the "weapons room"; each man was given as many weapons as he could carry to take with us to our temporary camp. It was not advisable to leave these weapons exposed to looters that were operating in the flooded towns along the flooded rivers. After setting up camp on the hilltops we had a rather easy time of it for a few days. We did have some duties to perform, but it was at a very relaxed pace until we could make "clean-up" details to work cleaning the flood mess. We had to keep the weapons that we had with us clean and oiled. We also had a field inspection of our personal tents.

Our Pup Tent and Gear

L to R; Dick Fuhr, Donald Bartling

Within a few days after the water receded, attempts were made to get everything back in order. The processing of the troops that were to go elsewhere was done quickly, and I found myself on orders to leave Ft Riley. My orders were a delay-in-route order to report to Ft Lawton Washington in eleven days. The next action was to go home and make plans for the "unknown" future.

CHAPTER 3

Pipeline to the Far East

Upon leaving the Ft. Riley Post a number of thoughts and emotions came to my mind. I first realized that I had learned a great deal about a number of things. I also realized that I had developed a degree of "feeling that this was a second home". Looking forward—there was the feeling that the time that had been spent there had been for a definite and worthwhile purpose. I felt a greater degree of patriotism than I had as little as a year earlier; I felt that whatever the future held, I had been adequately trained to meet the challenges that were almost certain to be a part of my life in the near future. Whatever the future held, I was determined to deliver the best of my ability.

Along with the preceding statements; I was also well aware that at the time there had become a sizable portion of the US population that were vocal about the wisdom of fighting a war in Asia, and also whether we could win it. This concerned me and my soldier friends considerably; as we felt that the effectiveness of the actions that were occurring, and that we would very likely become a part of very soon, were being diminished by the negative attitudes and actions of some of the American people. I realized that people that are comfortable develop a sense of "complacency" and seem to feel that they are entitled of a "life of ease and comfort". History shows us that eventually enemies of our Nation jolt them back to reality by some momentous action.

The events that had occurred since June of 1950 were evidence that the American people had again developed the attitude—that the Atlantic and Pacific Oceans were an adequate defense for our country. I did not agree with that evaluation. I felt that new developments had now made the continental United States increasingly vulnerable to devastating attacks.

I arrived at home and decided to utilize the days that I had before reporting to Ft Lawton, in a useful manner. I immediately determined that I should sell my car, as I did not want to store it for an extended period of time, and there was no need for it by the rest of the of the family. I was able to sell it within a few days. My friend, Dick Fuhr, and I decided that we should explore the possibility of getting a "free lift" from the Air Force for our trip to Seattle Washington. In order to accomplish this we went to Offutt Airbase, near Omaha, to find out what the possibility of doing this might be. Dick had a bright yellow Ford convertible that he offered to drive down to check this out. Needless to say we enjoyed cruising Omaha on a bright summer day. Dick's father was riding in the "rumble seat", and I think that he enjoyed it as much as we did. We found that—the ride would be available if they had flights scheduled for that day; however, we could not know until that day whether or not there would be a flight. Caution told us not to take a chance on reporting in late at Ft Lawton. We then went down to Union Station and bought our tickets on the City of Portland, a Union Pacific streamliner, so that our transportation was assured in a timely fashion.

On the night of August 12th the family took me to the Union Station in Omaha. I was met there by Dick and his family. We boarded the City of Portland for the beginning of the trip to Ft Lawton, Washington. Nearly all of the seats of the train were filled, so we would have plenty of company on our train trip. I know that there were some intense emotional moments that transpired at that time. For Dick and myself there was mixed emotions. One was the desire for the adventure of going to places that up until now we had only heard of, and the opposite emotion of the unknown dangers, responsibilities, and duties that may become a part of our futures. We knew that those feelings were also held by the families that we had just left behind. Because of the full passenger list on the train we had separate seats in different cars, so we had the contradictory situation of traveling together—separately.

The trip took us through much of the scenic Northwest US. We arrived in Portland Oregon about mid-morning of the second day, and transferred to the train that would take us to Seattle in a few hours. We had the good fortune that Dick's sister Eunice and brother-in-law Jerry Dunbar lived in the area and they met us at the train. They treated me as if they had known me for a long time and made us feel very much welcome in their home. Jerry insisted that they wanted to show us the sights of the area, so they took us on tour of the Seattle area. We were exposed to much of the area and enjoyed a restaurant meal with them. Jerry had said that he would get us to the Front Gate of Fort Lawton in time. He did with about ten minutes to spare. We were very grateful for their hospitality, as it made the time pass quickly and enjoyably. They were employees of Boeing Aircraft Co. so they needed to go to work during the week, but they invited us to another evening tour a few days later. We enjoyed it as much as the first tour and we were grateful for that evening too.

The processing of our records and issuance of our rifles (which we were to carry from this time forward) brought us back to the reality that we were not on a vacation; but that we were a part of an endeavor that was much larger than—just us.

On the afternoon of August 20th, 1951. We were informed that we were to report to a bus that would take us to a train that would take us to the airport in Vancouver.B.C. Our group of approximately twenty men were to board a Canadian-Pacific Airliner for Haneda International Airport, Tokyo, Japan that night. This plane was a 4-engine British plane. This was going to be my first plane ride as I had not ridden an airplane up until now. So it appeared that my first experience was going to be a long one. Most of the men in that group were men that we had trained with in Leaders Course. An unusual situation on this journey was that the CEO of the Canadian Pacific was escorting us from Seattle to Vancouver. Upon arriving in Vancouver we were placed on a bus that was to take us to the airport. He was with us on the bus and he said that he wanted us to see some of Vancouver, B.C. before we went to the airport; so he told the bus driver to take us to a number of the downtown sights of Vancouver and then took us to the airport. At the Vancouver International Airport, we were delivered directly to the plane and did not go through the Terminal; but there was a large number of people that had congregated near the plane. We picked up our duffel bags and rifles and proceeded to board the plane. To our surprise—the crowd that was gathered there gave us a cheer. With that kind of encouragement the prospects of the future were brightened considerably. The reality that events were moving very rapidly dawned on us at this time. We had fully expected about a two-week ride on a troopship, but now we would be in Tokyo before the ship left the United States.

It was an overnight flight from Vancouver to Elmendorf Airbase near Anchorage, Alaska. We had breakfast in a mess hall at Elmendorf. My first view of Alaska was the sun coming up over Elmendorf Airbase. I decided that if at all possible I would return, sometime in the future, to see more of this territory, as it appealed to my sense of exploration. After the plane was refueled and we had consumed our breakfast, we again boarded the plane for the next leg of our journey. This was to be to an outpost and airstrip on the Aleutian Island, of Shemya. Everything seemed to be going well as we cruised along above the clouds; however, we were to find out later that all things were not well at all. The planes radio equipment failed and it presented a problem in locating the airstrip in the fog that had developed near the surface of the ocean. The pilots brought the plane down to where it appeared that we would get our feet wet; suddenly, the plane darted upward. The airstrip had been found, but it was at an elevation that was higher than that at which we were flying. We landed on the next approach and the pilot informed us that we would be there until the radio equipment was repaired. We and the two stewardesses left the plane for a small lounge and dining area awaiting the call to reboard. We had a meal at this time. By now we had lost all relevance of date or the time of day, as we were near the international dateline and the calendar would add a day when we crossed it. After considerable time we were told to reboard the plane to continue our trip to Tokyo, Japan. We were quite sleepy by this time, so most of us dropped off to sleep. After some time we were awakened by the stewardesses. They felt that we should have the opportunity to view the sunset, as the sunsets are quite spectacular at that location. They were right—the view of the sun on the mountains and clouds on our right were indeed a sight worth viewing. We thanked them for waking us so that we could view the beauty of the sight. We soon went back to sleep and were awakened shortly before landing at Haneda Airport, Tokyo, Japan. It was after midnight Tokyo time that we left the plane and boarded a bus that took us to Camp Drake.

That we were now in a different climate and culture was immediately noticeable. August in Tokyo is hot and muggy, so we were somewhat physically uncomfortable. Apparently the local population was equally uncomfortable; as we observed a man cooling himself under an improvised shower right along the side of the street that we were traveling on. We were assigned bunks in a large barracks and tried to sleep the rest of the night. We were now aware that the calendar date was August 23rd.

The next step in our journey was rapidly approaching, as we were at Camp Drake only for a short time. Dick and I felt that the time had come to visit the Camp barbershop. It was staffed with Japanese barbers and we decided to get "the works". This included a haircut, shave, neck massage, and a manicure. We were in neighboring chairs and were entertained by watching the process especially the "neck massage". After our renovation we were able to attend a stage show that was put on by a group of Japanese Kabuki Dancers. We could not understand it, but it was something to pass the time. The show was about Japanese history, and included many colorful dragons. Each of these dragons had several people in them; they portrayed some event on the distant past of Japan.

Our next move was to the Tokyo Railroad Station where we boarded a train for Sasebo, Japan. As we had now turned in our dress uniforms and were issued back packs and the full field equipment that a field soldier needs; we presented a different sight than our transportation transfer in Vancouver B.C. Here, as in Vancouver, we were the center of public attention as we filed onto the train; we numbered well over one hundred men. Here the crowd just watched and hardly made a sound; it gives a person a rather weird feeling, knowing that between five and ten years before we were mortal enemies. This train was powered by a very old Japanese steam engine. It reminded us of the kind that we would see in the "western" movies, and with a very shrill whistle. This train did not travel very fast and as a result—we were greeted at nearly every crossing as we traveled through the countryside. The people that came out were the young children. It being August we were surprised to see them come out for the "gum and candy" handouts that the soldiers tossed to them from the train. Most of them were not wearing any clothing or shoes. This was another culture change that could not go unnoticed. The cars were equipped with wooden benches, that had been designed for smaller bodies than we were, so they were not the most comfortable to ride on for that length of time.

Japanese Countryside

Japanese Countryside

We spent very little time at the Sasebo Naval Base. We moved almost directly from the train to an ocean going ferry by the name of KONA MARU. The overnight ferry ride was a travel brochure event. We slept on the mat covered floors. Our packs were our pillows. On this particular night the Sea of Japan was without a ripple and the moon was very bright. It was a sight that would be remembered.

On the morning of August 28th we arrived in the Port of Pusan, Korea. We were immediately aware that we were now in a war area. In walking down the gangplank from the ferry, we could see the US Hope a US Hospital ship near a pier on one side, and a Swedish Hospital Ship on the other side near a pier. They also displayed a large Red Cross on each side. We had no need for anyone to tell us why they were there, we knew.

As we walked along the pier into a warehouse we were served coffee and donuts by the Red Cross. From there we proceeded directly to the train that would take us to our next destination.

The train that we boarded was in a very decrepit condition. All of the windows of this former passenger car had been shot out and were boarded over and the seats had been replaced with 3-tiered bunks. We tossed our packs up on our choice of bunk, placed our rifles nearby, and then hoisted ourselves into whatever level bunk that we would claim until the end of the railroad line. Door guards were chosen from the soldiers, one was placed at each end of each car. They were given ammunition, but the rest of us had no ammunition at this time. There were occasional guerrilla actions against trains of this kind. We were fortunate in that we did not encounter any of that during this trip. The steam engine was very much like the Japanese one in that it was very small and could have used more horsepower. The nearly open cars also were somewhat uncomfortable because of the smoke that came through, especially in the tunnels. We arrived at Chip-Yong-Ni at about sundown, were given chow and assigned a squad tent in which to stretch out and sleep for one night. At this time we were given our 7th Division shoulder patches and told to attach them before tomorrow. Even though we had sewing kits that we could use to attach them, we chose to hand our shirts over the fence to some Korean women that had come out to do this for a fee. We had turned in our U S coins and currency for scrip earlier in our travels. This scrip was issued in nickel, dime, quarter, half dollar, and one, five and ten dollar certificates. We paid our seamstress bills with this scrip. This was done to prevent the enemy from using American currency to purchase supplies that could be used against us in the war. They were very busy for a while.

We slept undisturbed until the next morning, which was August 30th. At this point we were divided into three groups. Some of us would be going to 17th Regiment, some to the 31st Regiment, and some to the 32nd Regiment, of the 7th Infantry Division. Dick Fuhr was assigned to the 17th and I was assigned to the 31st.

**Korean Woman Carrying
Load On Head**

Korean Papa-San

About mid-morning we were picked up by the trucks from our assigned regiments. This was going to be quite a long truck ride, so we were given some C Rations to use along the way. We went up through Chunchon and around the Hwachon Reservoir. Chunchon was a mass of ruble, and we saw very few people there. We arrived at the Regimental Replacement Center about five in the afternoon. We were about to see the front lines much sooner than was usually the case. A major assault had been made in the days

Chunchon Ruins

just past, and the drive to take some critical hills was having a great deal of difficulty. The Commanding Officer of the company told us to dismount from the trucks, fill our canteens at the lister bag (a canvass bag that held probably 50 gallons of water) that was nearby, place our packs in a tent, and report back to the trucks. It was not a feeling of anticipation for us "new men" to stand there, hearing the roar of the artillery, and being told to get on the trucks and go wherever they would take us. Our purpose was to go as far as the road would let us and then assist in carrying supplies up the mountain and assist the wounded down the mountain. We were given several clips of ammunition to use if events forced us to do so. At this time we had not even been assigned to our companies. We were able to get as far as the Heavy Mortar Position, which was the end of the road. The trail up the mountain was also there, as were several ambulance jeeps. It was dark by the time that we arrived at this point. The noise of the mortars, artillery, and rifle and machine gun fire was very loud. Also the searchlights were using the beams of light to reflect off of the clouds. This procedure made it possible for the troops on our side to observe the movements of the enemy. We were paired off and given a stretcher. The stretcher was loaded with supplies and we started up the trail. Surprisingly, in all of the confusion, we still managed to get our cargoes to their proper destinations. The supplies were unloaded, and the wounded would be placed on the stretcher for our trip down the mountain. This was a slow and tedious process, as the trail was rocky and steep. It took all night for me and my partner to make two round trips. On the last trip down we were met by a Chaplain that I was going to become much better acquainted with in the coming months. Father Lynch was a husky man and very capable in the job that he was doing. He had each stretcher stop a minute or so and he would talk to the man on the stretcher. He really gave the injured men a real lift in spirits. At daybreak the activity slowed and we were trucked back to the Regimental Replacement Company area. We were given our morning meal and then told to get some rest, as we had not slept in nearly 30 hours. Dick Beltz and I pitched our pup tent and tried to get some sleep. The events of the past days did not let us get to sleep easily; but we were tired enough to drop off for several hours.

We were to receive a refresher course in "patrolling" and "bayonet fighting" during the next days. We did that and on the 5th of September, Dick Beltz and I were picked up by the 3/4T truck from the AT&M Platoon of the Hq & Hg Company of the 31st Infantry Regiment.
I had been exposed to the reality of war during the past week: and it reinforced my long held opinion—that Communism had to be fought, and though there were many miscalculations by the U S Government that brought us to this point; we had to finish this so that our families at home would not be exposed to the type of devastation and death, of which we had only seen a small bit at this point.

CHAPTER 4

Actions—Fall of 1951

The driver of the truck took the men that had been assigned to the 31st Inf Regt to the Regimental Headquarters command post. Dick Beltz and I were told that we were being assigned to the Anti-Tank and Mine Platoon of the Headquarters Company. As they were at the time on a detail, the truck driver was told to take us to that location. This was late in the afternoon, and as our driver was also assigned to the AT&M Platoon, we were to proceed to the nearest point to the work detail as we could get before dark. After some time we reached the spot where we had been on the night episode of several days earlier. The Heavy Mortar Company had now set up on part of this location. Since it was so late in the day we stayed at this location overnight. The three of us slept in the back of the 3/4 ton truck.

Our sleep was interrupted several times during the night as the mortars were called upon for firing on the enemy that was attacking the front-line positions.

At daybreak we ate some c-rations and started up the mountain trail that would take us to the position that the platoon was working at that time. On the way up we encountered foot traffic coming down and we asked directions from some of them. One of those that we talked to was a Forward Observer for the Heavy Mortar Co. He was a great help in telling us just where

Loading Cable Car In Hwachon Area

to find our destination and the route that we should take to get there. There also was a mountain stream that flowed along the trail. Many GIs were filling their canteens from that stream. The forward observer told us that if anyone wanted to do that they probably should not proceed any further up the trail, as they would probably have a different view of drinking the water after they would see the dead Chinese soldier that was lying in the stream. We did not need any water, but we did see the Chinaman.

We arrived at the destination shortly before noon. The project that had been assigned to the platoon was the transferring of supplies from one tramway to another. The 13th Combat Engineers had constructed these for the purpose of moving materials faster and more easily. We reported to M/Sgt Ryan and then, as ordered by him, we pitched our pup tent; and then reported back to him for further orders. We were told that we would be taking our turns in the transfer process. This would only be done during the daylight hours, as the operators of the winches on the other ends had to be able to see us in order to start and stop them at the proper time. I was assigned to the 1st Squad with Sgt Rehfeldt as my squad leader. It took several days to get acquainted with the other members of the platoon.

After the first night on the front I decided that I would no longer keep track of the dates of importance. No soldier wants to become a prisoner-of-war, but if such an incident should occur, we did not want any information about troop strength or location to be found on our persons. Because of that decision, my dating of events is necessarily of an approximate nature. We were on this location about a week to ten days and then went back to the Regimental C P.

Our first project after returning from the tramways was to build a bunker for some of the Regimental Offices. This project would be my first in bunker building; it would not be too difficult as the basic skills that were needed were being proficient in the use of picks, shovels, axes, and crosscut saws. The farm boys, like me, were well prepared to handle those tools. As we were north of the 38 parallel we could cut any tree that we chose. We liked straight trees that had size for strength. We always saw to it that the tools did not get much rest, as it was almost a rule that we have two men for each tool. The real purpose was that, with this arrangement we could have half of the guys resting while the other half worked. I did not know it at the time, but I would have considerable use for the skill of bunker building in the months to come. These bunkers had to be able to withstand small arms fire, and the effects of the larger mortars that the enemy had. We used the excavated earth to fill the sandbags that were then placed around the exposed parts of the bunker to absorb the fire that it may be subjected to at some time.

Sfc Peterson was the Assistant Platoon Sergeant. He was the type of leader that the enlisted men under him admired and respected. He would not accept improper speech or actions by anyone. The men knew this and respected him for it. He always received the fullest cooperation from his men. He also was a good instructor. He did not want any of his men to be a risk to himself, his comrades, or the purpose for which we were there. As there were several new men (myself included) that had not had any training in the use of demolitions. He put forth extra efforts to teach us how to handle them safely and efficiently. The military at that time used a number of demolition materials. Our most used were TNT and C3. We also had Tetratol Chain Blocks, and Primacord. We had to

L to R., Don Bartling and Sfc Petersen

learn how to insert detonators, fuses, and igniters. We also had to learn how to determine which explosive and how much of it was needed for whatever problem presented itself. We also had two 3.5 in Bazookas, and a flame-thrower that used napalm. Mine detectors were a part of our equipment, but earlier experience had shown that they were almost useless. The ground had so much shrapnel in it after having been fought over four times in about fourteen months. Because of this the detectors were consistently giving false alarms; therefore, when mine clearing problems arose the men used bayonets to probe the ground in whatever area needed clearing. This operation usually required getting down on the hands and knees and crawling forward in a pattern, so that all of the ground was checked properly. This training was going to prove to be of great importance to us in the near future.

At this time we were located by the Hwachon Reservoir Dam. Our tents were right below the spillway. We did not feel too comfortable being that close to a dam that could be blown out. At the time we did not know that earlier in the war; we had tried to bomb the dam and spillway system unsuccessfully. It was much sturdier that we thought. Most of us pitched our pup tents a fair distance up the side of the mountain, as it made us feel safer.

Regiment Command Post, Hiwachon

M/Sgt Ryan rotated to the States in the latter part of September or early October, and Sfc Peterson was promoted to the position of Platoon Sergeant. Sfc Graham became the Assistant Platoon Sergeant. The Table of Organization called for a Lieutenant to be the Platoon Leader, but we had none then and did not have an Officer in that position during the time that I was a part of the unit. Also about this time I was promoted to Pfc. The fact that a promotion came through unexpectedly was gratifying, but my main objective was to do the job that was there for us to do and do so without injury or death.

At this time we would bathe and do our laundry in the river; however, we knew that we could not do this much longer as the weather would be turning much cooler. The laundry problem was solved very easily and unexpectedly. I never found out how the teenage Korean boys found us; but each unit would sort of adopt a washy-washy boy

Dick Beltz Washing Clothes

to do our laundry for us. Chan joined us sometime about the middle of October; he was fourteen years old. His parents had been killed by the

Chan

North Korean Army, an older brother was a soldier in the North Korean Army, and he thought that his sister was still alive, but he did not know where she could be, as he had no communication with her.

He was very good at doing our laundry down by the river. He would use hot water, as most of the soldiers used cold river water. Each one of us would pay him with scrip, and he was very good at taking care of his money. He could speak Korean, Japanese, and some English. His English improved steadily, and within a few months he could speak it fluently.

As was done in WWII, the Army Special Services Units arranged and brought entertainment to the troops. Our platoon was assigned the duty of preparing a suitable stage for the entertainers to perform. This was one of the "fun" things that we had the opportunity to enjoy. We had one in early October, but then we had to wait until the next spring for the next one, as the

USO—Special Services Show

weather became too unpredictable and cold for the performers to ply their trade comfortably. The troops always enjoyed these shows. It gave them a break from the pressures of their duties.

In the first part of October the 7th division and the 31st Inf Regt were ordered to move into the area of Heartbreak, Ridge, Bloody Ridge, and Mun-Dung-Ni. The 2nd Division had been battling the enemy there for nearly a month and they needed a break from line duty. The First Squad of the AT&M Platoon was detailed to be the advance party to prepare the REGIMENTAL HQ COMMAND POST for the rest of the unit that would follow within the next two days. We arrived at the location shortly after noon on a bright October day. The 2nd Division Replacement Co was immediately across the river from where we decided to pitch our squad tent. There was a 2nd Division Lt. that we reported to at that location. While we were engaged in conversation with him, there was an eruption of activity across the river. A Korean man ran out of a tent, followed by a U S Army Officer that ordered him to "Halt". He did not do so; and continued to run for the timber and mountain ravines. The officer shot at him with his .45 pistol, but the range was too great and he had no effect on the target. Sgt Rehfeldt, my squad leader, said to the Lieutenant—"Do you want him?" The lieutenant said, "Yes". Sgt Rehfeldt then said to us—"Bring him down". Six M-1 Rifles were raised and fired almost simultaneously. We will never know which one of us hit the target, but one of us did. He was placed on a truck and brought across the river, he was alive but the rifle bullet had penetrated from the back and exited near his heart. Whether he survived or not I do not know. This was my first experience at shooting at a human. I would rather not have had to do that, but apparently he was considered to be a possible spy for the enemy. With those circumstances, I could accept the fact that I may have been the one that fired the bullet that hit the target.

The next morning we observed the interrogation of a North Korean soldier by the South Korean Intelligence. It appeared that they felt that he had information that would be valuable to them. At first he was very uncooperative. We could not understand the conversation that was going on between them, but we could see that the "gentle" approach was not getting the results that they wanted. His attitude changed dramatically when a soldier came out with a rope and a water bucket. One look at that, and he sat down and talked to them for quite a length of time. It seemed as though they were satisfied with his answers, at least for this time.

We spent the next week or so in organizing the Command Post and getting the area functioning smoothly. Sfc Graham and I were detailed to check out some suspicious munitions that were found by one of the Security Posts on the top of a ridge about one-half mile from the Regimental CP. It turned out to be rather simple—the munitions were some abandoned 81mm mortar rounds. They were disposed of in the proper manner. We were about to find out that it was not always that simple or easy to handle the assignments.

About the first of November the Regiment received orders to use some aggressive action to make the line stronger and more easily defended. In the process of carrying out those orders, the 31st Tank Co. was deployed to take control of a valley area near Heartbreak Ridge and Mun-Dung-Ni. They were met with strong enemy resistance and had to leave a disabled Sherman Tank about one-half mile in enemy territory. There was the body of a US soldier in the tank. The next morning AT&M was ordered to accompany the tanks in an effort to recover the tank and body of the man in it. We started up the valley with an infantry squad (10 men) on the right and an infantry squad on the left of the line of tanks. AT&M men were on the ground probing for mines directly in front of the first tank. One-half of the men were probing and the other half were taking cover over the river bank. They would be put into action if the need arose. We were encountering some sniper fire and an occasional mortar round. The enemy had planted many mines in the valley over night and previous to this time. It was a scary experience that I find difficult to describe. The tanks were firing the 50Cal machine guns and 75mm cannon almost continuously. The mortar rounds were falling quite close to us and the small arms fire was whizzing around us. As the mines were found they were disposed of by placing a TNT charge on them and detonating it. The enemy was using wooden boxes with the explosive charge detonated by a pressure fuse. They had about 12 pounds of explosive in them; this was sufficient to blow off a track and bogie wheels of a tank. They had two pressure settings. With the small wooden slide gate closed—200 pounds were required to detonate it, with it open 2 pounds would detonate it. We had been asked to clear a rather broad area, as the tanks wanted to be able to maneuver and direct their cannon fire to the right, up another branch of the valley. I and several other probers were just off the left side of the leading tank when the enemy released an intense mortar barrage. At this time there was utter chaos, as the noise of the battle also now included the voices of the wounded and the dying men. I was probably 8-10 feet away from Cpl. McSpadden and he died within a few minutes. Several of the riflemen were also wounded. Immediately we were ordered to pick up the dead and wounded and return to the Tank Co CP. At this point eight of our AT&M Platoon men were awarded the Combat Infantryman's

Badge for satisfactory performance of duty under enemy ground fire. I was one of the eight. These badges were distributed to us about a week later. Because of rotation and other attrition our unit had become rather inexperienced because we had not been subjected to the rigors of battle. At this time I felt (and many of my comrades also) that we were a very small part of a very much larger picture. Many agreed with my feelings that we were alive because of the grace and protection of the Almighty God. At this time I realized that I was there for a purpose and I wanted God to lead my actions, so that I could do what needed to be done with efficiency and honor. Within a few weeks we would all be battle-hardened soldiers, as we had only begun a campaign that would call for many more days just like this one. We were saddened by the death of our comrade, even though he had only been with us about a week. I was fully convinced that the Almighty had control of every bullet and piece of shrapnel out there and could therewith protect anyone that He chose from any and all dangers. This confidence really helps when one is working with detonators under battle pressures. Nervous hands are a danger as steadiness is necessary when a person is handling detonators. We were sent back to our tents and told to be ready for another attempt the next morning.

We reported to the trucks the next morning for transportation back to the 31st Tank Co CP. This was to become our routine for nearly every day for the next two weeks. I do not remember nor do I want relate each day of activity during this time, but I will touch on several events that might illustrate how wars are fought. The features of this particular location became very familiar to all of us as the weeks progressed. We knew where every rock pile, rice paddy, and trench was located. As we advanced up the valley with our mine clearing details, we had to look into each trench very carefully before trying to cross over them; because the enemy had on occasion crawled into the trenches from the other river bed and replaced the mines that we had dismantled. One day we had worked from the early morning (about 8 o'clock) until past three in the afternoon and we were getting heavy fire from the ridge on our left. Our problem was suddenly solved by a flight of Mustangs that delivered napalm bombs to the mountainside. The entire mountain was suddenly in flames and our problem from that section was completely gone. There was mixed feelings as those Mustangs flew over us at a height of maybe one hundred feet and we could see the napalm bomb suspended from the undersides of them. Those pilots were very accurate in their release of the bombs; a few seconds too soon and we would have been the ones getting burned, a few seconds too late and the target would have survived the attack.

One day Sfc Peterson was sitting in a shell crater and observing how the operation was going. He sat there for maybe an hour and as he rose to leave he glanced back at the spot where he had been sitting; to his surprise he noted that he had been sitting on the top of a tank mine the whole time. Fortunately, that one was set for the 200 pound detonation setting.

Another day of activity showed the dedication and courage of the American soldiers. We had found a number of enemy mines and because of the closeness to the working men we delayed blowing them up until the men had been given the opportunity to withdraw from the immediate area. After retreating to a safe distance Sfc Peterson gave the order to detonate the charges that had been placed on the located tank mines. Two TNT charges were placed on each mine (we used two to insure that the detonation did not fail). We stayed low as several of the men pulled the igniters and headed for cover. In about two minutes three explosions occurred. Sfc Peterson asked—Was that all of them? Did we miss some? Or did they explode simultaneously? The only way to be certain that all of the charges had detonated was for someone to go back the entire distance and check them out. Sfc Peterson and the squad leader from the infantry cover squad decided that they would be the ones to do this. We had experienced considerable fire up until this time, and it looked like they would be walking into a very dangerous situation; to our amazement—as they walked out in clear view of the enemy and started toward the enemy lines—the firing ceased completely. They walked all of the way out, found the undetonated charges, pulled the igniters, and calmly started walking back to our lines. The charges exploded and the project was a success. Sfc Peterson received the award of a Silver Star for the bravery that he demonstrated that day. The other soldier may also have been given an award. Of that I do not know. Within the next day or so Sfc Peterson was rotated back to the United States; his platoon was going to miss him, but they also knew that he had earned his trip home.

With the rotation of Sfc Peterson, Sfc Graham became our Platoon Leader. Most men would rather take over a command at a time of relatively low activity. Sfc Graham was not about to have that privilege, as we were to try again the next day. It had become commonplace that as the trucks that transported us to the Tank Co would come around a bend in the road we would get a barrage of mortar fire from the enemy. This morning was no different; we were met with an unusually heavy barrage. The trucks were brought to a hasty stop and the men dived into the ditches or whatever cover we could find. No one was injured in this episode, but Sfc Graham was presented with a problem that no commander of troops wants to experience. Two of the men complained of illness and did not want to proceed any further. He had a difficult problem to solve immediately. He announced that he would deal with these two at a later time, and that if there were volunteers to fill their places he would place them in those positions and proceed with the assignment. I hesitated for an instant or two, and then decided that the spot where we were was not really a safe place either, and the mission must be completed. I then volunteered to be one of the needed men and a man I had only met a few days earlier, Dale Moffitt, said that he would also volunteer. We then went into action and had a successful day insofar as casualties were concerned. I later would be able to depend on Dale in many tough spots.

One other event that was of interest was the action that occurred near the end of our series of patrols. We had advanced very rapidly that morning and it appeared that we could get our tank retriever up to the disabled tank that we had set out to recover many days earlier. I and another member of our platoon were forced to take cover in a shell hole momentarily. As we looked over the edge of the shell hole we could see the mortar rounds exploding in a pattern that was almost certain to put some in our shell hole within a few minutes. There was another shell hole that offered better protection about thirty feet away. We decided to try for it. He went first and arrived safely in his new shelter. I started to raise up on my hands and knees in order to make a dash for the same hole, when a round hit the edge of the shell hole and really stunned me. I maintained my thoughts and tried again; I had barely cleared the top of the shell hole when a round fell in the hole that I had just rolled out of.

I knew immediately that I had some ear damage from that situation, but was grateful that I could continue to be effective. If the ground had been level there, I would have had the same fate as Cpl McSpadden received earlier during this campaign. From that point on the action that morning failed to accomplish our objective, so we would have to try again at a different time as the fog was beginning to settle in and we could not accomplish anything with the fog in the area. We withdrew and then had another event that turned out all right, even though we could have had some unnecessary casualties had we not recognized the group of men that came out of the ravine on our right as we came back into the Tank Co area. The Korean Service Corp (a Korean Civilian Service group) had delivered hot food to the men on the line behind us and were returning to the mess tent where it had been prepared. They did not recognize us in the fog and we did not recognize them. Our lead men saw them move and alerted all of us to bring our rifles to bear on them. All of the rifle bolts slammed into position and were ready for firing when the Korean Lieutenant that led them spoke in English and relieved the tension. We were ready to remount the trucks and call it a day.

A review of the actions of this period showed that none of us could tell exactly how many times we had attempted to recover the disabled tank. There were a number of casualties by all of the units involved—both WIA and KIA. Also there had been several tanks that had to be recovered because of the tracks being blown off of them. We were very grateful, that though we were tired and had cuts and bruises, we were alive and well. Also the Infantry Co to the right of the valley was virtually wiped out as they tried to take the hill to our right. Nearly half of the two hundred men in that company were KIA during this time.

As the weather became wetter and colder we actually prayed for cold weather so that we could not penetrate the ground with the bayonets and would force a close of this operation. On Thanksgiving Day, the weather did as we had hoped and we were not required to go into that valley again.

As the winter was showing signs of closing in and the memories of the severe winter of the preceding year was still fresh in the minds of all of the troops; we decided to take special precautions to keep ourselves warm it the coming months. The squad tents were regularly equipped with two fuel burners; but we decided that we were going to back that up with a wood stove that we manufactured from a fuel drum and artillery casings. We could burn wood and waste paper in it. One day we noticed that there was a fuel drum that had apparently fallen off the fuel truck and rolled some distance down the mountainside. We checked it out and found that it was full of gasoline. We immediately made plans to salvage it for our own use. This operation would require some coordination and muscle. It was located on a pass that was a single file of traffic controlled by the Military Police. Five of us

L to R., Sgt Zerfing and Cpl Horam Cutting Wood

went down the mountain and we placed another traffic controller of our own in the pass. The MP`s could not see him or each other so it required perfect timing for the fuel barrel to be on the road at the time that our two and one/half ton truck came through the pass. We only had a few minutes to load it or the MP`s would be wondering why the traffic was not flowing steadily. We were a well coordinated group and we managed to pull it off without a hitch. From this time on we would put our empty drum on the fuel truck with the rest of them and we got our refills regularly.

In early December Capt Haggart replaced Capt Harris as our Company Commander. Capt. Harris had been a good CO and we hoped that we could be fortunate a second time. We were— Capt.Haggart was a top CO. He took a genuine interest in all of his men and was always abreast of the events and

Don Bartling On Tent

needs of the day. He would visit us in our tents regularly. One day he came in and said that he had a detail for the new Cpl to carry out for him. I was the new Cpl, and I wondered what this detail could be. He informed us that we were going to be moving soon. The tents were anchored with wooden stakes, and with the frozen ground it would be next to impossible to drive the wooden stakes. He had requested two cases (140 pounds each) of drift pins. These were steel pins that were 20 inches long that we could drive in the frozen, rocky soil. His request was denied and he felt that we did not have the time to run it through the process again. He felt that the individual that made the decision on this did not understand the problem. He asked me to take two husky men and the jeep and get some for our use. I will say that with some conniving and daring we acquired the needed materials. This type of procedure is not a regular occurrence; but unusual methods are sometimes necessary in extreme circumstances.

Cartoon of Don Bartling's Promotion to Corporal

Within a few days we received the order to move and we were ready and able to make the move efficiently. This new location was very near the front lines, but was considered to be a well protected area from the enemy artillery.

CHAPTER 5

Actions—Winter of 1951-1952

The move to the new location was accomplished easily as the distance was short. The weather also cooperated with us making the ride comfortable.

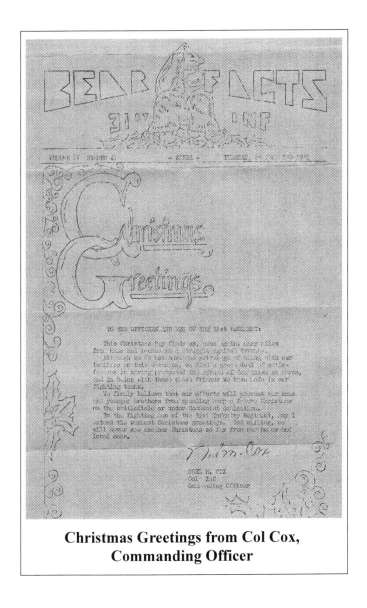

**Christmas Greetings from Col Cox,
Commanding Officer**

Soon after arriving at this location, Capt Haggart informed us that we were being asked to make an open-air and warmed chapel before Christmas arrived. The important event was that Cardinal Spellman of New York City was going to be there on Christmas Day. We had a platoon conference and brainstormed as to what we could do with what we had to work with. We made a platform and covered it with a squad tent that we erected with four long tent poles instead of two poles. This arrangement gave us the open-front that was desired. It required some extra ropes

Christmas Tree at 3rd. Bn Hq, 1951. (Beer Cans for Ornaments)

and stakes to secure it, in the event that we had a strong wind blowing into it. We also placed two stoves in the back corners to remove the chill from the air in the enclosure. It had a south exposure and we hoped to have some energy from the sun to also add some heat to the structure.

Outdoor Chapel Built for Christmas 1951—view 1

Outdoor Chapel Built for Christmas 1951—view 2

On Christmas Day we did not get the sunshine that we had hoped for, but the temperature was reasonably comfortable (around 25 degrees Fahrenheit). We had no wind to contend with so in spite of the feel of impending snow, the event had no weather problems.

At about ten o'clock in the morning the event began. General VanFleet, General Ridgeway, General Lemnitzer, and Cardinal Spellman arrived in one jeep. There were around one thousand men assembled in the Regimental Command Post area. The security had been increased and many of us were assigned to be on the perimeter of the crowd, to react should the need arise. Everything worked well and this was declared a successful event.

Jeep Carrying Cardinal Spellman, Gen Van Fleet, Gen Ridgeway, Gen Lemnitzer

Troops Gathered for 1951 Christmas Mass By Cardinal Spellman

At midday a large Christmas dinner was served to all of the troops. It was as welcome as the Thanksgiving dinner had been a month earlier. The menu was—roast turkey, mashed potatoes, vegetables, rolls and dessert. Our company had an outstanding kitchen staff and they served the troops very well.

Later in the afternoon of Christmas Day the snow started to come down very heavily. It forced a U S Marine helicopter to land there to avoid crashing into a mountain. Fortunately, it was able to take off early the

next morning. Had it not done so it too would likely have been hit by the enemy artillery that—on the day after Christmas at exactly the same time as the large crowd had been assembled there—the enemy did manage to drop an artillery round in the center of the assembly area. The guard that was patrolling the front of the CP was killed immediately. Why the round

fell at the time that it did was a matter of much discussion for some time. The unanswered question was, and remains, had enemy intelligence been off by one day?

After the Christmas Celebration, activities settled down to doing the routine things that are necessary to be combat effective should the need arise. At midnight on New Years Eve the U S Artillery sent a New Years Greeting by way of a volley of artillery. Those of us that had not known about the planned barrage were jolted awake by the intensity of the barrage. It was so intense that the vibrations shook all of the ashes out of our wood stove.

One night a few days later we were again reminded that the enemy could hit us with artillery. This time it was in the form of an air burst. Our tent was the hardest hit by that burst. Dale Moffitt had gone to bed in his sleeping bag and a large piece of shrapnel hit his foot. We took him down to the aid station where they kept him for two days. He was quite lame when he came back, but he was very grateful that there was no permanent damage to his foot. He also appreciated the fact that he or someone else was not hit in a more damaging fashion. He later joked about getting a Purple Heart while he was in bed. He called it the lazy way to get one, but deep down we all knew that he would have preferred not to have been in a position to receive one.

The morning after the artillery hit, our "tent repairman" (Diaz) got out the repair kit and sewed and glued patches over the holes in the tent. His civilian occupation had been with carnivals and he had acquired considerable knowledge about tents. He also had to repair some holes in some of the surrounding tents.

A few days after that we were working with some captured enemy munitions and a captured machine gun. It was my day for a small misfortune. Some of the detonators exploded a little too close to me and I caught

Sgt Don Bartling and a Captured "Chink" Machine Gun

some of the shrapnel. I had to have a piece about the size of a 22 cal bullet removed from my left thumb. I had other scratches also but they were of no consequence. I was asked to apply for the Purple Heart, but I refused as I did not feel that I could accept the same award that some of my personal friends received for giving their lives. Also many of us felt that the news of such an award would be very upsetting to the families at home.

We also had some humorous events that occurred from time to time. At about noon one day Chan returned from doing some laundry down by the river. He was an unusual sight in that he was wearing a pile cap, a field jacket, long johns, and boots. We asked him where his pants were and he answered this way. Put gas in can, spilled some on pants, light up match, Whoosh!!, pants have-a-no. We found it hard to believe that he had not burned himself in the least. We found him another pants and his routine returned to normal.

Near the end of February the effects of the rotation were becoming very apparent in our platoon. M/Sgt Graham and Sfc Rehfeldt along with a number of other platoon members rotated to the United States. This required a reshuffling of the platoon command and the replacement by new personnel. In this process I found myself being promoted to Sgt and given command of the 1st squad.

A few days before Sgt Rehfeldt rotated home, he decided to tease some of the other platoon members. After noon chow on a warm February day he started to throw the melting snow into the tent through the air flaps. Several of us in the tent did not appreciate getting showered with the wet snow. I decided to retaliate. I gathered the snow that he had thrown into the tent into a large ball about the size of a basketball. I positioned myself just inside of the tent door and when he came in I smashed the snow down on the top of his head. I should have known that this would precipitate a reaction. The reaction soon found the two of us in a wrestling match inside the tent. After some time we decided to call off the struggle and forget about it. Needless to say the inside of the tent was a royal "mess".

A near disaster was averted on another day when we were called upon to get our shovels and use them to put out a fire in a tent. The ROK detachment that was working with our Security Platoon was housed in an "Arctic Tent". This was an insulated tent, but a stove was also necessary to make them comfortable on cold days and nights. They upset the stove and the gasoline was pouring out and saturating the entire tent and the contents of it. The tent was enveloped in flames almost immediately. Our main concern as we approached the burning tent was the possibility of the ammunition and grenades exploding because of the fire. We shoveled the snow as rapidly as possible and the possible explosions did not occur.

In early March we were again on the move, this time to location south of the 38th parallel. At this location we would occasionally see some of the South Korean civilians. This required that we treat them in a proper manner.

Since we had at this time a number of new replacements that had not fired their weapons, Capt Haggart asked me to take the entire platoon for a march out to a ravine a mile or two down the road. This ravine was being used as a firing range. During the winter we had convinced the powers that be that we would be more efficient in our mine clearing duties if we had 30 cal carbines instead of 30 cal rifles. Because of this change in weapons practically none of us had fired the carbines. Many other units were using this range so we were given an allotted time for us to use it.

This location also was adjacent to a cemetery. This cemetery had a few gravestones, but most of the graves were under earthen mounds. As we were coming in I posted a range guard who was not to allow anyone else in the area during our time there. I had not even had time to get the men to the firing line before Pfc Carey called out that he had a problem. In looking back we could see that he was being accosted by a Korean woman that was carrying a bowl of steaming hot rice in each hand. She was threatening to throw the hot rice on him if he would not let her pass. I immediately changed the order and he let her pass. I told the platoon that there was a change of plans—instead of firing our weapons we would get a lesson in Korean culture. The woman then proceeded to a certain mound. She placed one bowl of rice on top of the mound and proceeded to eat the other one. After she had eaten the first bowl of rice, she exchanged the bowls and ate the second bowl of rice. The time required going through that ritual was about thirty minutes.

She then left, and since our time was up we also left. Our firing exercise had to be postponed to a later time as the next group was already there. I inquired of Chan that evening as to the purpose and significance of this woman's actions. He said, "She came to bring some food for the departed person's spirit". I asked him if the spirit could eat the food. He countered with a question of his own. He asked, "What do Americans do on the cemeteries"? I answered that we place flowers there as a symbol of the eternal life of the soul of the person. He then asked me this question, "Can they smell the flowers"?

At this location we also became acquainted with the Colombian Battalion. They were attached to the 31st Regiment. Our tents were adjacent to each other and since some of them could speak English and we had some that could speak Spanish, we developed a measure of friendship. I observed at the time that, though we were engaged in an action in which we had a common purpose, the language barrier does present some problems from time to time. This was going to present itself to me personally within a month or so.

The peace negotiations at Panmunjon were going on during this entire period. They had arrived at a conclusion as to where the Demarcation Line would most likely be placed. Our platoon along with the like platoons and the

Mine Clearing

Combat Engineers received orders to remove all mines in an area about three hundred feet wide across the entire country. We were to mark this area with engineer's tape on each side. Since there was considerable snow on the ground and the ground under it either rocky or frozen this exercise could not be very efficient, but we did it anyway.

I also picked up a copy of the psychological flyers that we distributed over the enemy from time to time. The end result was that most of this could be done without fear of enemy fire, as they just watched us go through the motions. Most of the work was ignored after a few weeks or months.

**Psychological Warfare
Flyer
(front)**

**Psychological Warfare
Flyer
(back)**

We were then given the job of erecting a pre-fabricated building. With the expertise of the two carpenters in the platoon and the help of the rest of the platoon we erected it in a very short order. It was quite different working with dimension lumber as compared to the logs that we used for the other construction that we needed from time to time.

In early March Capt Haggart informed me that I was being appointed Assistant Platoon Sergeant and Sgt Dyke was to be the leader of the first squad. One of my first duties in this position was to make an exploratory trip to the next location that we would be moving to very soon. This presented an opportunity to begin the education of the men that would be following me, when my rotation time arrived. As protocol requires—I was in the right front seat as that is where the ranking person is required to be. In the back of the jeep was a corporal that showed promise of being a very effective soldier. We needed to travel a considerable distance on the MSR (main supply route) and there were many military units along the way. Each had a gate guard position near the road. As we traveled along we were getting salutes from almost all of the guards as we passed by. Archie remarked—Sarge, this is a lot of fun, I like getting saluted like this. In looking back at him I realized that he was wearing our Polar Bear Crest on the epaulets of his field jacket. It was immediately obvious that we were giving the impression of that there was a person of quite high rank in the front seat of that jeep. I told him to remove the pins and we would find out whether we were still considered important. He followed instructions and as expected the fun was over. After some time Archie spoke up again—Can I put my crests back and really test this theory. I permitted it and the fun times resumed. We completed our inspection trip and returned to prepare for the next move.

The move to Inje was accomplished without incident and we set up camp away from the front for the first time in many months.

One of the first work assignments that we received at Inje was to build a fancy Regimental Entrance. It seemed rather unnecessary to do this, but that decision was made by someone else, so we constructed it complete with a banner.

Regimental Entrance

**Sfc Lawrence
"Picadilly"
Zerfing**

At this time (early April) my turn for Rest and Recuperation leave came up. Many of the fellows chose to refuse this opportunity to see some of Japan. I felt that I could conduct myself in the proper manner, and that it was an opportunity of a lifetime to see more of the Japanese country and culture. With this break in both the activity and the weather this appears to be a likely place to close this chapter.

CHAPTER 6

Actions—Spring of 1952

With the regiment in reserve and no pressing problems or projects that required immediate attention, there could not have been a better time than this for a vacation. This was designed to relieve some of the pressure that builds up during stressful periods. How beneficial it was depended largely on the individual that was utilizing the opportunity. I was determined to make it a learning experience.

A short distance from our command post was the ruins of a church. I do not know who built it, but I do know that the Catholic church had been quite active in parts of the country in some years past. All that was left of the structure now was the walls and stone floor. The roof had been burned off sometime in the past year. This church was the assembly point for the men going on R&R from this regiment.

Whenever there is an activity of any kind, there is a need for the "orientation period". In this case the orientation was presented by the Chaplain and the Chief Medical Officer of the Regiment.

The chaplain spoke first. His message was that we should try to present ourselves in Japan as honest and moral persons. He stressed the moral part as it was the area in which the most problems arose. The medical person then spoke to the men, and in effect said that he endorsed everything that the chaplain had said—but that he did not expect a very large number of the men to conduct themselves in that fashion. From the reports that we had gotten from the men that had gone before us, we knew exactly the behavior pattern that he was referring to.

The trucks that were to take us to the airport at Chunchon arrived, and we were on our way to Yokohama, Japan. The airport at Chunchon was located on the limited amount of flat ground surrounded by fairly steep mountains. The weather had to be ideal for the cargo planes to safely use this airport. On this day the conditions were ideal and the C-54 cargo planes were able to take off easily. We needed to make one refueling stop at Osaka, Japan, this was done without incident and we arrived in Yokohama, Japan after dark of that day.

The processing of a group of this kind was very rapid. We turned in our field uniforms and headed for the showers. The shower was a treat in itself, as most of the men like me had the opportunity for only a shower or two over the time that we had been in Korea. We were issued Class A uniforms and then were allowed to go wherever we pleased. The Army had provided a place for this purpose—it was called Camp McNeely. The capacity for sleeping numbered in the hundreds—but most of the time the space was unused as the people that could have been there were housing themselves in the Japanese Hotels. I had a quonset hut that had around forty bunks in it all to myself. To me the clean fresh sheets were a treat also, as I had not slept out of my uniform since late in August. There was no charge for the bed and food that was consumed at this place.

The next morning I went several huts down the street to the mess hall. Here again I found the dining hall empty except for myself. I had the privilege of ordering a complete breakfast from a menu that included every breakfast item imaginable. I also had the exclusive service of two waiters. I was not the only person that ate there that morning—some came earlier and some came later—but it was never crowded.

Yokohama Skyline from Camp McNeely

As I was leaving the mess hall I noticed a 7th Division soldier walking toward me in the street. We met and introduced ourselves to each other. It turned out that Pfc Lemmert and I had very similar ideas as to what we wished to see and do on this leave. I had been given a sizable sum of money by Cpl Shum from my platoon. He had requested that I use it to purchase a reasonably good camera and case for him. He said I should use it on the R&R and deliver it to him upon my return to Korea. With this to be done, we decided to go downtown Yokohama for the day and try to make the purchase. We made the leisurely walk down to the area where there were numerous shops of all kinds. These were usually quite small, but no space was wasted in them. Some were specialty shops—such as, silks, paintings, silver engraving, etc. Others were more retail outlets for many items. We leisurely explored the shops as they were on the street; whatever came next we would go into and see how the markets operated here. The exchange

Pfc Everson Lemmert

rate at that time was 360 yen to the dollar. The prices were posted in yen, so a buyer had to do some mental mathematics to convert the prices to dollars. Also the posted price was never the selling price—all prices were set by negotiation. After some time we came to a camera shop. We were not experts in the camera field, so we had to look more intelligent than we probably were. After some time we thought that we had a fair idea as to what I should buy and the price

Sgt Don Bartling

that I would be willing to pay. I made an offer on the one that I planned to buy. This started the negotiations. It became a process of who would cave in first. After some time we settled on a price and the purchase was made. Many of these items could be purchased at the Yokohama Post Exchange (PX), but it was more fun doing it this way.

We found that the PX also had a very good soda fountain. Their malted milk shakes were an attraction that we gravitated back to at least once every day that we spent in Yokohama. We spent the rest of the day just exploring the various shops and then returned to the mess hall at Camp

McNeely. The "day room" there was named "Club Chotto Motti" which means something like No 1. We spent some time there reading some books and papers and listening to the radio. About nine o'clock we decided to call it a day as we wanted to go to Tokyo the next day.

We met at breakfast the second day and inquired from our waiters as to some tips about going to Tokyo. They provided some very helpful tips on the travel, location of points of interest, also areas that were undesirable. It helped us to use our time and money much more efficiently.

Day Room

We went down to the Railroad Station and took the high speed electric train for the trip to Tokyo.

The electric train to Tokyo was an interesting experience. It ran on a very strict schedule and there usually were more prospective passengers than there was passenger space. To utilize the space the most efficiently the railroad employed "pushers". They were very quick and active men that would push the crowd onto the train just before the door closed. We learned real soon that—you get on quickly and move to the far end immediately. In about thirty minutes we were at the Tokyo Station.

We felt that one of the important and interesting places would be the "Ginza". This street was the equivalent of Times Square in New York. There were many restaurants, shops, bars, and the main attraction there was the Ernie Pyle Theatre. We had not been to the movies for a long time so we took advantage of this to see some of the newer American movies. We saw several during the time that we were there.

Another point of interest was the Imperial Palace that was near the government center. There was a moat around it and the entrance was large, but was closed with a heavy wooden gate. We could not see much of the interior as it was enclosed with a stone wall.

The Diet Building was the center of the Japanese Parliament. It was a more modern building that visitors could walk up to but could not enter. In this area was the headquarters of FECOM. We knew that all of our orders passed through that headquarters and they had a great influence on the events that affected us personally.

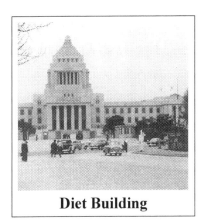

Diet Building

Diet Building

Also along this street was the Ginza Park. Some of the park still showed the effects of the fire bombing that the U S Airforce had delivered in 1944 and 1945. It was also evident that the vacant lots were the result of that same event. A shrine was also along this street, but we did not know, or learn, the history of it. As we had been advised to avoid the train rush hour, we caught the train back to Yokohama and decided to come back the next day to see more of this interesting place.

**Statue In Ruins
of Park**

Japanese Shrine

The next morning we retraced our route to Tokyo. We spent more time just viewing the architecture of the buildings, and the activities of the people that were out and about in rather large numbers. They all seemed to have some reason to be there, and many of them appeared to be

Pedicab

working in that area. We felt that no trip to Japan would be complete without a pedicab ride. We had no special place to go, but going nowhere was still an experience that we enjoyed. With two people in the seat the pedaler had to work very hard on the upgrades.

I inquired about the location of an address that I had of the LCMS Japanese Mission in the area. The distance to it was not that far, but I wondered about getting a taxi driver to understand where I wanted to go. It was not a problem as the printed address was all that he needed to find the location of the Mission. I told my friend that I planned on going there and he immediately said that—if I didn't mind, he would like to accompany me. I was agreeable to that and we engaged a taxi and went there. I was much surprised upon arriving there that we were in for an enjoyable and educational time. A Rev Bergt was the person in charge of this mission at that time. Surprisingly, he also was a Nebraska native, so we had much in common as to the discussion of our home state. While we were visiting with him, his wife baked a chocolate cake and served us some of it. That was an item that neither one of us had enjoyed since we left home. He also invited us to the Good Friday church service that was to be held at 7:00 P.M. We were scheduled to be back at the R&R center by midnight of that night. We told him that if we could make the travel work out that we would attend. He said that we should not worry about it. If the taxi could not get us there on time he would find someone that could take us there. It being late in the afternoon, we decided to return to Camp McNeely in Yokohama.

We decided to spend the next two days in Yokohama. We wanted to purchase some souvenirs for our family members at home. We definitely wanted items that had significance so we spent considerable time in searching for and purchasing the items that we wanted to send home. The Yokohama PX had a packaging and mailing service that we wanted to utilize. This service made the process of mailing very easy. We also spent some time on the top of the PX. There was a Japanese garden up there along with refreshment counters. We found it to be a relaxing place and we could imbibe in more malted milk shakes.

Yokohama Street Scene

**Sgt Bartling and
Pfc Lemmert
In Japanese Garden**

Late in the afternoon we engaged a taxi to take us back to the LCMS Mission. The Good Friday Church Service was a memorable event. It was for me the highlight of the whole R&R experience. Rev Bergt had seen us sitting in the back row of the chapel. In the closing prayers of the service he included us with a statement that we were going back to Korea that night. As we left the chapel we were met by about twenty fellow servicemen of all ranks that wished us well as we left. To me that was a very humbling experience, but also highly appreciated.

Upon returning to the R&R center we prepared to go back to Korea. We turned in our dress uniforms and replaced them with freshly laundered field uniforms. We were to take off from Yokohama before daybreak. Here again my front

**C-54 Troop Transport
Kimpo Airport, Seoul**

of the alphabet name placed me on the first flight out. Ordinarily, that would not have been of any consequence, but this time it was. Shortly after we were airborne the announcement was made that we would be the only flight going to Chunchon. The weather was fogging in the airport there and if we could not land on the first pass we would have to return to Japan. The rest of the R&R people were given an extra day in Japan. As the time passed the plans were changed again. This time it was—make a pass at Chunchon—if we could not land—proceed to Kimpo Airport in Seoul. Just about dark on a cloudy day we landed in Seoul.

We were issued a package of C rations and then we bedded down in the bombed and burned out railroad station. It was reasonably warm so with the number of people crowded into a room we were fairly comfortable as we slept that night. There was no roof over our heads so we could have plenty of fresh air. The next morning was Easter Sunday and we were told to eat some of the rations and be prepared to get on the trucks that would take us back to Chunchon and Inje. We heated our sausage patties on the truck engine exhaust manifolds, and soon were ready to go.

Seoul Railway Depot Wreckage

It was a sunny morning and the temperature began to rise early in the day. It was a trip through the war wrecked city, and most of the countryside that we passed through that day also showed the effects of the war. We returned to Inje in time for evening chow.

War Torn Seoul

War Torn Seoul

War Wrecked Factories

Early on Monday morning Capt Haggart came to our tent. He asked me to come out to talk with him. I had been the manager of all of the platoon activities for some time. This was because the Platoon Sgt had asked me to do this. During the week of my absence he decided that he would rather not be in that position any longer. Capt Haggart asked me if I would be agreeable to accepting the role of Platoon Sgt. Since I was doing the work anyway—I agreed to do that.

During the week of my absence a POW enclosure had been constructed quite close to our tents. It was a timber and barbed wire structure. The only use that was required of it in the time before our next move was to use it as a holding place for our washy-washy boys. Regimental Intelligence had determined that there could be some information being passed to the enemy during the nights by these boys. They were taken further south and released. When Chan went into the enclosure he said to me—" do not worry about me, I will be all right". After a few days I was lying on my cot after noon chow, the tent walls had been rolled up because the sun was very welcome in the tent. I was suddenly surprised by a hand touching my elbow. I reacted rather quickly and here was Chan. He said to me—"got anything to eat?" I gave him some cookies and candy bars. I asked him how he found back here and where he was staying. He said that he had read the numbers on the trucks and then hitchhiked back to a place further down the river. After a few more days, most of the washy-washy boys were back to their original places.

While we were at this location, the Third Battalion was up the road about a quarter of a mile. They had their flag out along the MSR (Main Supply Route). They wanted to have retreat ceremony at 5 P.M. every day. Since I needed to teach my new men how to use explosives this presented an opportunity to show them how it was done, and also to give them some hands-on experience. We would take a block of TNT and cut it into smaller pieces, insert an electrical cap, and detonate it by connecting to a battery with communication wire. It was placed down in the sand by the river and detonated at the proper time for the Battalion to have their retreat ceremony and lower the flag. All of the new men had the opportunity to fire off at least one charge during this time period.

Some of the men captured a young deer one day. They intended to make a pet of it, but after about a week of tending to it, they decided to release it again as there was more work to tend it than they wanted to do.

In the first week of May we were ordered to move up to the Kumwha area. I also received my Sfc stripes at this time.

The geology of the Kumhwa area was very different from any that we had been in previously. The valleys were wider and the lower hills were of a coarse gravel soil. The mountains surrounding these hills and valleys were just as steep and rugged as any that we had encountered earlier. We were going to become well acquainted with much of each in the next weeks.

At this location we were to live in bunkers instead of tents. We turned in our tents and cots and moved to the new location. The units that had been there previously had done a super job of bunker building, and they were equipped with built-in cots for sleeping. We were about to begin a time of having many projects to complete in a relatively short time.

Command Post Bunker

Sfc Don Bartling

We were ordered to build a bunker about 25 feet long and 20 feet deep. I (and several other farm boys) looked at the assigned location with a high degree of skepticism. As farmers we could recognize a spot that would very likely have a spring under it. The person that decided to put it there insisted that the only place that it could be placed was on that exact spot. We followed orders and built it in a few days. Because of the dampness we even placed gravel on the floor. Within a few days the weather turned a little wetter and the spring started to make the bunker a mess. Now they wanted to know how to correct the problem of the excess water. A number of artillery shell casings were available at the Field Artillery Battalion. We acquired a number of them, took them to the motor pool to punch holes in them, and dug a trench inside of the bunker around both sides and the back. The casings were placed in the trench and covered with gravel with a fair drop from the rear to the front. The system worked and we claimed to have the only bunker in Korea that had running water.

It was evident that there was planning for some action in the near future. Defenses were being strengthened, and new ones constructed. One afternoon I was instructed to have two squads of men on a ridge looking toward the enemy positions about a half mile away across the valley. We were to bring pickaxes, shovels, and sand bags. We arrived at the appointed location shortly after noon. The Captain from the operations section was there to tell us what he wanted done. At some time earlier a cut had been bulldozed through the ridge. The Captain wanted us to make a sandbag barrier across this cut. It was to be about five feet high and four feet wide. This was to be a firing position for a tank that they wanted to use as direct fire artillery from that location. We went about our work (knowing that we were under enemy observation) and tried to expose ourselves as little as possible. We had some artillery go over us that afternoon, but none of it came close to us, and we were able to complete our project without any problems.

During this time we often had night patrols between the lines. Our purpose was to remove any tank mines that we could find in the area close to Porkchop Hill. Since we were working at night, the procedure of disposing of the mines was to defuse them. We did not want to disclose to the enemy that we were out there by exploding them as we would do in the daylight. Several times we also accompanied a company of Combat Engineers that enabled us to clear a much larger area in a given length of time.

An article in the Stars & Stripes told about the enemy using information taken from POWs to blackmail the families back home. Upon learning of this practice, we started leaving everything that might identify our families in the U S, with trusted friends when we went on these patrols. We just wore our dog tags for identification.

At this time the military was experimenting with body armor (flak jackets). The Army had several units that transported a number of these jackets along the front. They would bring them to the units that had a high likelihood of being under fire. We were one of the first units to have them for our use. We wore them, but fortunately, we did not give them a test. We never drew fire of any kind during these patrols. The jackets were turned back after we returned from the patrol. It was a little scary defusing the mines in the dark. We did it by feel most of the time.

One early evening in early June I and the first squad leader, Sgt Dyke, went up to the line company opposite of Sniper Ridge. The Capt there was to show us the area that was in front of the company. Sgt Dyke's squad was to clear the area that night. By this time most of the ridges had trenches dug along the entire top of the ridge. The Capt took us along the entire area. On our return trip, I stopped to take a quick look through a machine gun emplacement. I had hardly stopped when there was a loud "Crack", I looked behind me and the sand was running out of a sandbag. The shot pattern was only about two inches in diameter. The Capt turned and said to me—"I forgot to tell you that they have been trying to hit that machine gun all afternoon". It was nice to know that but I wish that I would have known it a little sooner. Sgt Dyke and his men accomplished their mission without incident.

Another incident that worked out well was a night patrol that I had some early reservations about. Capt Haggart came out to our bunker building project and told me to send half of the men to the bunkers to rest up for the night patrol that was scheduled for the coming night. As he explained to me where we were to go I developed some concerns. I told Capt Haggart that I had problems with the route that the higher powers had outlined for us. My problem was with their plan of having us return through the Colombian Battalion. The Colombians were very good soldiers, but they were especially trigger-happy at night. Also the use of "passwords" was almost impossible. I felt that it was safer for my men to retrace our steps after we had reached our objective than to try to come through the Colombian lines. He agreed with my premise and volunteered to go with me to see the Regimental Executive Officer. We knocked on the door of the Majors Van. The Major had a reputation of being a person that was difficult to deal with. He opened the door. Capt Haggart introduced me and told him that I had a problem to discuss with him. He said—You have two minutes to tell me your problem. I explained my concerns, and he said—All right do it your way, but it had better work. On the way back Capt Haggart said to me—If this does not work, which platoon do you want in A Co tomorrow morning? I replied—I will worry about that in the morning Sir. A Co had been almost wiped out a few days before and was being reconstituted at the time. Again we accomplished our mission without incident and no more was said about it. Every operation of this type had two requirements that had to be met. 1. Do all that you can to accomplish the mission, and 2. Do not put your men in any more danger than is absolutely necessary.

At this time we were asked to construct another much larger bunker, and also construct a metal frame for the briefing tent. With both of these projects being done at the same time we had to use all of the manpower that we had every day.

Constructing Briefing Tent

Completed Briefing Tent

Sfc Don Bartling on Bunker Construction Project

One day after I had assigned the three squads the work for the day, a runner from the Co CP came to inform me that I should report to the CP. I did and was told that there was a probable mine problem at the Service Company. Since all of the men were busy I decided to go down and check it out myself. I used a jeep to go to the Service Company. I was met by a soldier when I arrived. He said that he would show me what the problem was. He took me into his tent and showed me a small wooden box that he had noticed next to his bunk. He had reason to be concerned as this was an enemy anti-personnel mine that we called "shoe mines". If detonated it would amputate a man's leg at the knee very easily. I told him what it was and suggested that he remove himself to a safe distance as I was planning to defuse it. He was either "daring" or more inquisitive than he should have been, as he insisted that he wanted to watch me do the defusing. It went well and I dismantled the mine. He then talked to another soldier outside of the tent that said—" I have one of those beside my truck wheels". I then asked my first friend if he would ask around for more information on the possible location of more of these little "firecrackers". I soon had a detail of eight or nine men that helped me look over the entire company area. We found a few more and they too were taken care of by defusing. I found a lot of new friends that day.

On about the first of June my platoon was assigned a new responsibility. One of the men of the 31st had (while in a drunken state) punched an officer. He was awaiting a court martial, and he had to be somewhere until the trial was held. Capt. Haggart felt that he was not about to go anywhere and we could use the muscle power in our projects so he sent him to us. I felt like we had also become a "guard house", but we made the arrangement work.

Also about this time I had an addition to the guard house portion by one of my own men. This was a very disturbing occurrence. I had given permission to part of the men to go down to the Service Company to view a movie on a screen that they had set up there. I had allowed this on several other nights. All went well until upon their return they went into the other ATM bunker to settle in for the night. The rule was that "all weapons must have a clear chamber in the company area". One of the men forgot about it until everyone was in the bunker. He then stated—I wonder have I cleared my carbine? He then proceeded to slide the bolt back and forgetting that he also had a finger on the trigger. The weapon fired. The bullet struck another of my men and killed him almost instantly. The bullet also traveled to one of my ROK men and passed between his arm and his rib cage. He had burns on both the rib cage and his arm but otherwise unhurt. I now had a major problem to contend with. I sent for Capt Haggart and Lt.Kim. Lt Kim was able to interpret for us what his three men had to tell about the incident. I immediately felt that the most accurate account of the tragedy would be available—NOW. I set up a table, got paper, and pen, and asked each person in the bunker to come down and give a deposition. This process took about two hours. I then turned my information over to

Capt Haggart. I began to wonder if this incident would have an impact on my rotation schedule. My position could require me to be there for the "courts martial". This situation could not be resolved in any other fashion. Time would prove that my concerns were unfounded, as when my rotation time came up, I was allowed to leave before the trials were even held.

The last few weeks of my time with the 31st were very busy ones as we had the building projects, and continued patrols right up until my last day with the Platoon and Company. In the end I had to leave without even having the opportunity to speak to each of the men in the platoon. I regretted that, as they had been a group of men that I was very proud of, and I would have preferred to thank each one personally. As it was, all that I could do was to write them a note and have someone read it to them later in the day.

Capt Haggart had asked me during the last month who I thought would be the best choice for Platoon Sgt after I would leave. I suggested Sfc Zerfing, so I expect that he is now the Platoon sergeant.

CHAPTER 7

Rotation Back to the States

On the morning of the 27th of June, I was handed my copy of the orders that ordered me back to the States. This proved to be another time of very mixed emotions. These emotions are held internally, and those around you are probably very unaware of their even being in existence. The strongest was the anticipation of going home, and a sense of gratitude that I had survived the previous ten months. The opposite feeling was—that the job was not finished, and all of these men that had worked with me were not going along with me. Overriding this whole scenario was the fact that—for all practical purposes the war was at a stalemate and would probably not be settled for a long time to come.

We boarded the truck that was to take us to the railroad. There was a significant difference from the train that brought us to this place. These cars had seats and were pulled by a diesel switch engine. The trip to Inchon was accomplished in a comparatively short time.

The time that was to be spent in Inchon was determined by the time of the arrival of the troop ship in the Inchon harbor. I really do not remember how many days that we

**Starting To Inchon
From Chorwon**

waited for the ship to come in. Even though we could still hear the heavy artillery from there, we knew that it was a very secure place to be. We turned in our personal weapons at this time and it had a rather unsettling effect on some of us. I felt that I was to a degree—naked. It bothered me the most at night as I did not have a weapon within reach while I was asleep. It took several days to adjust to the changed status. I especially was bothered by having absolutely nothing to do. All we did was eat and sleep. At the snack bar there I took my change in the Korean won. This note was almost worthless.

On the 3rd of July we boarded a LSI (Landing Ship Infantry) and rode out to a floating dock from which we walked up the steps to the deck of the ship. The 4th of July was spent sailing on the Yellow Sea. The ship arrived in Sasebo Japan on the 5th of July. We were to spend some more time there in processing for the ship ride that we were to take on the Gen Collins. Some of our time was spent in using our passes to downtown Sasebo. We also had various "orientation" sessions. About a week later we boarded the Gen Collins and set sail for Camp Stoneman, in San Francisco, California. We were to spend fifteen days on this ship. The weather was very calm except for one night of a severe thunderstorm. Many of the troops were seasick by morning, and the sun and calmer seas were very welcome. I was fortunate in that my bunk was near the center of the ship. Because of this location the wave action was not as severe there as it was in the bow and stern of the ship. I was fortunate in that I did not get seasick.

Camp Mower   **Administration Building**   **Japanese Shinto Shrine**

Ready To Board Ship
Gen Collins

Port of Sasebo

We arrived in San Francisco Harbor in the late afternoon. The Bay Bridge was a welcome sight, and since the weather was clear we had a good view of the San Francisco Skyline as we sailed up the harbor. We also had a good look at Alcatraz as we sailed by. We disembarked and were taken by bus to Camp Stoneman. The preliminary processing of the incoming troops took several hours. After evening chow we could make phone calls home. There was a large group of phone booths available, but with that many men that wanted to use them, it was some time before I was able to make a phone call to Hooper NE. It was a call that I had looked forward to for some time. The same was true of those at home that were wondering just when my ship would come in. We then turned in for the night.

Ready To Leave Ship In San Francisco

Alcatraz Island

The next morning we were back at the processing for our next leg of the trip to our homes. We were also given the opportunity to avail ourselves of some monetarily attractive reenlistment bonuses. At this point there was not much interest in even talking about that, as everyone was much more interested in getting out on the 30day leave that was waiting for us.

By late afternoon the group that was headed for Ft Carson, Colo. was taken by bus down to the railroad station. At this point my name position became evident again. Even though I was a Sfc I still was among the highest ranking of the men on this train. I was called to "front & center" and was informed that I and the next alphabetically listed Sfc were going to be responsible for the foot locker that contained all of the service records of the men on the train until we delivered them in Ft Carson. The promotion procedure had been frozen for some time and therefore many of the Sfcs would have been Master/Sgts if they had been given the rank that their positions authorized. This assignment in effect made me the equivalent of First Sgt of the train. This was not going to be a difficult position as the anticipation of getting home on leave made the troops very cooperative and congenial with each other. The fact that we had sleeper cars made the trip a relaxing one, and the arrangement that I outlined for them—of each car getting their turn to be first in the dining car was accepted and followed very well. The following afternoon we had a short (20 minute) layover in the Station in Salt Lake City. Most of the men had exhausted their supply of candy and cigarettes and would like to replenish their supply. I had been told that I was responsible that every man be on board when we arrived in Ft Carson. I told them that I would allow them a few minutes in the station if they would get on the train immediately when I signaled them from the station door. The operation ran like clockwork and everyone was on board with some time to spare. With cooperation like that—my job was not at all difficult. We would not get off of the train until the next afternoon in Ft Carson. This trip had given the men the opportunity to see the Great Salt Lake, and some of the best of the Rocky Mountain Scenery. We were met in Denver by a team of personnel processors. They relieved us of the records and started to work on them in a van as they traveled to Ft Carson.

We arrived in Ft Carson late in the afternoon. We were billeted for the night, served chow and turned in for the night. We were promised that we would be on our way to our homes about noon the next day.

The promise was good and about noon I went to the railroad station in Colorado Springs to get on a Rock Island train for Lincoln and Omaha. On this train I met Sfc Ed Faltin of Scribner, NE. We had not known each other prior to this time, but this meeting began what was to become a lifelong friendship. I left the train in Lincoln as I had been told by the travel agent that there would be a bus that I could use to get to Fremont at that time. The information was in error as the bus would not leave until late in the morning. Because of this I hired a taxi to take me to Fremont.

Monument & Railroad Station, Colorado Springs, CO

I arrived in Fremont sometime after midnight. My parents and sisters Erma and Vera met me there. Erma was rooming at our aunt's house, they wanted me to come in and visit them for a few minutes before coming on home. While there my mother asked me if I had gotten my Bronze Star yet. I had to answer that I knew absolutely nothing about that. I was informed that Capt Haggart had sent a letter with that information enclosed. I had not expected anything of that sort to be waiting for me at home, but it was.

HEADQUARTERS COMPANY 31ST INFANTRY
APO 7

23 July 1952

Sfc Donald G. Bartling
US 55077134
R R # 1
Herman, Nebraska

Dear Sergeant Bartling,

It is with great pleasure that I forward you a copy of the orders awarding you the Bronze Star.

I want to add my personal thanks for the way you worked for the Regiment and the Company.

Your devotion to duty was superior, and throughout my time in the Army, I have met very few men that could meet the high standard you have set. I know that you will be as successful in your civilian position as you were in the Army.

I thought you would like to know that Sergeant Zerfing has the platoon now, and will be going home as soon as I can get a promotion for him.

Best regards to you and your family.

JACK F. HAGGART   Inf
Capt
Commanding

Bronze Star Letter From Capt Haggart

3

HEADQUARTERS
7TH INFANTRY DIVISION
APO 7

GENERAL ORDERS   20 July 1952
NUMBER   297

Section I

AWARD OF THE BRONZE STAR MEDAL.--By direction of the
President, under the provisions of Executive Order 9419,
4 February 1944 (sec. II, WD Bul. 3, 1944), and pursuant to
authority in AR 600-45, the Bronze Star Medal for meritorious
service in connection with military operations against an enemy
of the United States during the period indicated is awarded to
the following-named officers and enlisted men:

Captain DAVID M. BULLOCK, 01119156, Corps of Engineers,
United States Army, in Korea, Company D, 13th Engineer Combat
Battalion, 2 January 1952 to 8 July 1952. Entered the Federal
service from Missouri.

First Lieutenant REMI F. MORIN, 02201228, Artillery, United
States Army, in Korea, Battery B, 31st Field Artillery Battalion,
19 November 1951 to 24 June 1952. Entered the Federal service
from New Hampshire.

First Lieutenant GILBERT C. SEPULVEDA, 02207386, Artillery,
United States Army, in Korea, Battery A, 57th Field Artillery
Battalion, 29 January 1952 to 12 May 1952. Entered the Federal
service from Texas.

First Lieutenant BARNEY W. SLAYTON, 01031025, Armor, United
States Army, in Korea, Company B, 73d Tank Battalion (Medium),
20 September 1951 to 30 June 1952. Entered the Federal service
from Michigan.

Sergeant First Class DONALD G. BARTLING, US55077134, Infantry,
United States Army, in Korea, Headquarters and Headquarters
Company, 31st Infantry, 2 September 1951 to 27 June 1952. Entered
the Federal service from Nebraska.

Sergeant KENNETH E. GROSS, US52054314, Infantry, United
States Army, in Korea, Company H, 31st Infantry, 27 October 1951
to 19 July 1952. Entered the Federal service from Ohio.

Sergeant MELVIN T. SANDERS, RA18264182, Infantry, United
States Army, in Korea, Headquarters Company, 2nd Battalion, 31st
Infantry, 2 September 1951 to 7 June 1952. Entered the Federal
service from Texas.

Corporal DOUGLAS HUGHES, US52139202, Infantry, United States
Army, in Korea, Company G, 31st Infantry, 29 August 1951 to 2 June
1952. Entered the Federal service from Kentucky.

General Orders for Award of The Bronze Star Medal
page 1

GO 297, Hq 7th Inf Div, APO 7, 20 Jul 52

Corporal DEMPSEY B. LATHAM, JR., US53052252, Infantry, United States Army, in Korea, Headquarters Company, 2nd Battalion, 31st Infantry, 11 September 1951 to 17 June 1952. Entered the Federal service from North Carolina.

Corporal JAMES J. McKINSEY, US52071427, Artillery, United States Army, in Korea, Headquarters Battery, 49th Field Artillery Battalion, 11 September 1951 to 12 July 1952. Entered the Federal service from Pennsylvania.

Corporal JOHN THOMAS, JR., RA16371848, Infantry, United States Army, in Korea, Company G, 31st Infantry, 9 September 1951 to 2 May 1952. Entered the Federal service from Illinois.

Private First Class WILLIAM G. MAASS, JR., US55036445, Infantry, United States Army, in Korea, Company G, 31st Infantry, 8 August 1951 to 28 May 1952. Entered the Federal service from Minnesota.

Section II

AWARD OF THE BRONZE STAR MEDAL (FIRST BRONZE OAK-LEAF CLUSTER).--By direction of the President, under the provisions of Executive Order 9419, 4 February 1944 (sec. II, WD Bul. 3, 1944), and pursuant to authority in AR 600-45, the Bronze Star Medal (First Oak-Leaf Cluster) for meritorious service in connection with military operations against an enemy of the United States during the period indicated is awarded to the following-named officer:

First Lieutenant DONALD W. CARRUTH, O1297496, Infantry, United States Army, in Korea, Company K, 31st Infantry, 1 April 1952 to 15 July 1952. Entered the Federal service from Vermont.

BY COMMAND OF BRIGADIER GENERAL WAYNE SMITH:

OFFICIAL:

ROYAL REYNOLDS, JR
Colonel, GS
Chief of Staff

L. E. SMITH, JR
WOJG, USA
Asst AG

DISTRIBUTION:
A Plus
TAG ATTN: AGAO-I (4)
     ATTN: AGPO-A (3)
CINCFE ATTN: AG-DA (2)

EUSAK ATTN: KAG-MD (1)
IX Corps (2)
PIO (1)
En individual concerned (5)

2

**General Orders for Award of The Bronze Star Medal
page 2**

HEADQUARTERS
NEBRASKA MILITARY DISTRICT
FEDERAL OFFICE BUILDING
OMAHA 2, NEBRASKA

12 November 1952

SFC Donald G. Bartling
Herman, Nebraska

Dear Sergeant Bartling:

I have the honor to inform you that, by direction of the President of the United States, the Bronze Star Medal has been awarded to you for meritorious service during the period 2 September 1951 to 27 June 1952.

This headquarters has been directed to select an officer to present this decoration to you at an appropriate ceremony in accordance with your wishes. The decoration may be presented to you in your home in the presence of friends and relatives, or should you desire, the presentation may take place at a meeting of a Veterans Organization, or any other place you may select.

If you do not wish a formal presentation, the medal can be sent to you by registered mail without attendant ceremony. It is our desire to be guided by your wishes insofar as practicable.

Please inform us as to your wishes in this matter. A self-addressed franked envelope, which requires no postage, is inclosed for your reply.

Sincerely yours,

L. V. CLOSSON
Major, AGC
Adjutant

1 Incl
  Franked envelope

HEADQUARTERS
7TH INFANTRY DIVISION
APO 7

AWARD OF THE BRONZE STAR MEDAL

Sergeant First Class DONALD G. BARTLING, US55077134, Infantry, United States Army, a member of Headquarters and Headquarters Company, 31st Infantry, distinguished himself by meritorious service during the period 2 September 1951 to 27 June 1952. During this period, Sergeant BARTLING peformed his duties as a Combat Construction Foreman in an exemplary manner. He supervised the construction of bunkers, trenches, gun emplacements, and other field fortifications, and the clearing of mine fields. Much of the construction was accomplished under enemy observation and fire. His coolness and courage, coupled with his sound tactical judgement, earned him the respect and confidence of his men. His conduct marked him as an outstanding soldier. The meritorious service of Sergeant BARTLING reflects great credit on himself and the military service. Entered the Federal service from Nebraska.

OFFICIAL:

L. E. SMITH, JR
LOJG, USA
Asst AG

Award Of The Bronze Star

When I arrived at home I was met by my "old dog friend" Bruno. I never saw a dog wag his tail more energetically than Bruno did. I know that he really wanted to welcome me home.

One of my first desires was to visit brother Harvey in Ft Riley, Kansas. He was finishing his basic training at about this time. I spent two days there and then returned home.

Within a week or ten days I had purchased a new 1952 Ford automobile. With these new wheels I was able to go wherever and whenever I pleased; but I spent most of my time at home. This was a very happy time except that I could tell from the daily newscasts that my AT&M platoon had again been exposed to some very dangerous actions. They were involved in the taking of Pork chop Hill. I later learned that Cpl Shum, (the man that I had purchased the camera for) was killed in that action.

L to R, Harvey and Donald Bartling, Aug 1952

During this month, Harvey began the Leaders Course and I knew that he was very busy. He did manage to come home on the final weekend of my leave. As he needed to be in Ft Riley one day before I was to report in Ft Carson, we arranged to give him a ride to Ft Riley and then Sfc Edward Faltin and I traveled on to Ft Carson. I was then ready to finish my active army career within the next six weeks.

CHAPTER 8

Completing the Tour of Duty

We reported to the incoming personnel department, and were sent up to the billeting office. To my surprise we were met by a friend of Ed and mine—Sfc Gilbert Kriz of Dodge, NE. He asked me if I had been assigned a duty station yet. I said that as far as I knew, I had not been assigned. He informed me that there was a position identical to his (Charge of Quarters) that would be open within a few days. He introduced me to M/Sgt Forbes, the unit First Sgt, and suggested that he request an assignment for me at this location. The duties at this place were to answer the telephone and be available during the day for errand duty. After the regular hours closed at five in the afternoon the CQ had to be there for anything that might arise until seven the next morning. This was a 24 hour stretch of duty. The night man was given an assistant—and most times that helped to pass the slow moving hours after midnight. The person then would get 72 hours off duty before he had to report for duty again. This sounded quite attractive to me as I hoped to explore the sights of Colorado during this time period.

Within a day or so I received the assignment to be a CQ at the Billeting Section of the Replacement Center. I had a cadre room in one of the nearby barracks to sleep in, so I felt very well fixed.

One morning Sgt Forbes requested that I come by as he had a problem that he needed help to manage. When I reported to him, his first question was—"Can you handle a .45 Pistol?" My answer was—"Yes, as I had carried one for a short time and was very familiar with it". He then brought out a belt and loaded .45 Pistol. My assignment was to escort an AWOL (absent without leave) soldier to get him re-equipped with clothing, as all that he had was the clothes on his back. He had been in the army almost eighteen months but had only served about three weeks. He was an expert at slipping away. I went down to the Guardhouse and presented my credentials. They were expecting me and they brought out the man in very short order.

I informed him that we were going to get him some clothes, and that if he behaved himself this should not be a difficult activity. I ordered him to get out in front of me about four paces and to walk in the middle of the street. His method of escape had been to get in a crowd of people near buildings so that he could duck out of sight and the guard would not dare to shoot at him. He asked—"Would you shoot me if I tried to run away?" I replied—"Do not test me by trying. You are a very big target". He started to march as ordered and no attempts were made to escape as we marched over a large part of the camp. I returned him to the Guardhouse fully equipped to face whatever duty that he would be assigned to do. This was not my preferred duty, but I had long ago learned that you do what needs to be done, even if you may not like it very well.

To offset this type of duty, there are humorous events that occur frequently. One of my fellow CQs had been sort of intrigued by the voice of one of the telephone operators at the telephone center. We talked to them many times a day. He said that he sure would like to meet her, but he was skeptical of asking for a date without seeing her first. He said she has such a young sounding voice. He asked if I would drive him down to the parking lot near the telephone center. He knew her name and that they wore name tags. He inquired about the time of the shift change and we drove over to the parking lot. We started to walk down the sidewalk toward the building at the same time that a group of the telephone operators came toward the parking lot. As we met he shoved his elbow into my ribs and said—"Keep on walking". After we had moved out of hearing distance I asked him what the problem was. He answered—"If the name tag was right the rest of the lady is not nearly as young as her voice." That incident foreclosed any more travels to the parking lot near the telephone center.

Everyone is liable to make a mistake from time to time. It seems that I made a real big mistake while on CQ duty one night. I should have recognized the situation for what it was—a prank. Ordinarily, we were informed at least 12 hours before a group of soldiers would be coming through. This time I received a call after midnight that two planeloads of soldiers was coming in to Peterson Field within an hour or so. I referred the caller to the Incoming Office and waited for instructions from there. Later I received the second call reiterating that the troops were coming in soon. I had several options to follow on this and I chose the wrong one. I called the Motor Pool and informed them of the information that I had received. I should have called my superiors and had them check it out. At about eight o'clock the next morning, I was awakened by a knock on my room door. The information was that I was wanted to report to the First Sergeant immediately. Upon reporting to him I was informed of the fact that I had triggered an unnecessary trip of the buses to the airport. I admitted that I was the person that made those calls and the reason why I did it. Sergeant Forbes sent me back to my room for some sleep and ordered me back to talk to him at one o'clock. I had told him that I recognized my error and that he should do whatever he had to do—which could include a rank reduction. Upon reporting to him he told me that the Major had checked my service record and found it clean and that there would not be any action taken in regard to my error. A day or two later, I noticed that the person that I had suspected of instigating the problem had lost three grades and also his position.

With the work schedule that I had it was easy to find at least one day out of the three days off to do other things. Sfc Faltin and I traveled to the Garden of the Gods, Seven Falls, Cave of the Winds, Pikes Peak, and other sites that make this area a tourist attraction. I also found it easy to use some of my spare time to take GIs to Denver when the regular means of transportation was not available.

Sfc Faltin

The time passed rapidly and on the eleventh of October I was transferred to the Inactive Enlisted Reserves and I headed for home as the active time of my service was over. I arrived at home about 9 PM that evening. I was happy to find that brother Harvey had also come home with orders to report to Ft Lawton, Washington to begin his trip to his new duty station in Alaska. Although we had been officially transferred to the

Enlisted Reserve status, we still were required to report in to the 5th Army Office in Omaha. This was done within a few days.

In early November I received a letter from Major L. V. Closson in regard to the presentation of the Bronze Star Medal. I chose to go low key on this and with my parents accompanying me we went to the Omaha Office of the Nebraska Military District. I think my parents were more enthused about observing the presentation than I was. I felt then and I still feel today that though I am happy to have received it, there are probably many more that should have received it, but did not. It is times like this that reminded me that—success in the military is accomplished by the "little bits" of numerous individuals. Many times in the decades of the 40's and 50's they numbered in the millions. I also realized that I owed a great deal to many of my fellow servicemen, both at that time and in the many times in our history in which the life and future of the Nation was in peril.

The last event that was of importance to me was the receipt of my official discharge certificate on August 30, 1956. It gave me a different outlook as to how I could conduct my future activities.

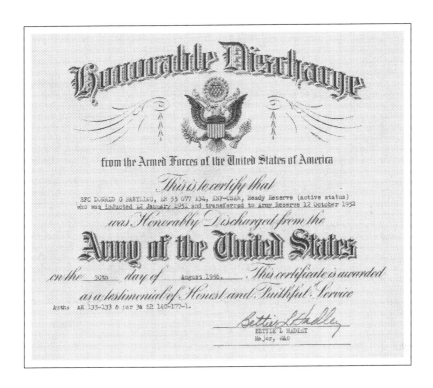

This had appeared to be the close of my military recognition until 50 years later the Government of South Korea issued a Medal to all of the men and women that had a part in the War from June of 1950 until July of 1953. I can speak for myself and those that were fellow recipients that we do appreciate the recognition, even though the objective of a United Democratic Korea had not even then been accomplished.

Korean War Service Medal

Awarded On The 50th Anniversary Of The Korean War

감사 서한
Letter of Appreciation

대한민국
THE REPUBLIC OF KOREA

Letter Of Appreciation
Page 1

존경하는 참전용사 귀하

　6·25전쟁이 발발한지 반세기를 맞아 세계의 자유 민주주의와
대한민국을 수호하는데 기여한 귀하에게 진심으로 감사드립니다.
아울러 고귀한 생명을 바치신 영령앞에 무한한 경의와 추모의
뜻을 표합니다.

　대한민국이 오늘날의 자유 민주주의 국가를 유지할 수 있도록
귀하께서 보여주셨던 불굴의 신념과 진정한 용기, 그리고 거룩한
희생정신을 우리는 가슴속 깊이 간직하고 있습니다.

　특히 귀하께서 50년전에 몸으로 실천했던 자유민주주의 이념은
이제 새로운 세기, 새 천년을 맞아 세계 인류의 보편적 가치가 되
었습니다.

　이에 6·25전쟁 50주년을 맞이하여 귀하의 명예를 드높임과 동
시에 과거 혈맹으로 맺어졌던 귀하와의 우의를 재다짐하고자 합
니다. 아울러 인류의 발전과 평화를 위해 세계 우방들과 함께 노
력해 나갈 것입니다.

　다시 한번 귀하의 숭고한 헌신에 깊이 감사드리며 행운과 건승을
기원합니다.

　감사합니다.

2000년 6월 25일

대 한 민 국 대 통 령　　김　대　중

Letter Of Appreciation
Page 2

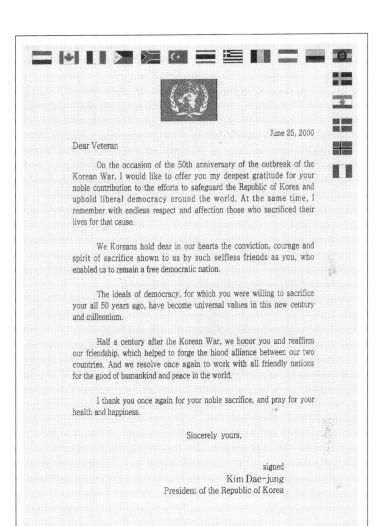

June 25, 2000

Dear Veteran

On the occasion of the 50th anniversary of the outbreak of the Korean War, I would like to offer you my deepest gratitude for your noble contribution to the efforts to safeguard the Republic of Korea and uphold liberal democracy around the world. At the same time, I remember with endless respect and affection those who sacrificed their lives for that cause.

We Koreans hold dear in our hearts the conviction, courage and spirit of sacrifice shown to us by such selfless friends as you, who enabled us to remain a free democratic nation.

The ideals of democracy, for which you were willing to sacrifice your all 50 years ago, have become universal values in this new century and millennium.

Half a century after the Korean War, we honor you and reaffirm our friendship, which helped to forge the blood alliance between our two countries. And we resolve once again to work with all friendly nations for the good of humankind and peace in the world.

I thank you once again for your noble sacrifice, and pray for your health and happiness.

Sincerely yours,

signed
Kim Dae-jung
President of the Republic of Korea

Letter Of Appreciation
Page 3

6·25전쟁 50주년
THE 50th ANNIVERSARY OF THE KOREAN WAR

Letter Of Appreciation
Page 4

CHAPTER 9

Overview of Events and Their Relation to the Present

In writing this history of the events of the period, I found that I regularly found myself trying to relate the experiences of that time for comparison with the occurrences in world and national affairs that have transpired during the last fifty-plus years. It is very apparent that conditions change, but human nature does not change.

Many times in the history of mankind the people have been called upon to make sacrifices so that the rest of the people around them can enjoy a safer and more comfortable living. This is especially true when the next generation is brought into consideration. I can refer to the period of WWII as a time when the people were fully aware of the dangers that confronted them. They had to be jolted out of their complacency by an attack that affected them personally. The attack on Pearl Harbor had an immediate effect. They then rose to the occasion and built the most powerful military machine that the world had ever seen up until that time. The cost in lives and national resources was the greatest that this nation had ever seen. We have not seen a similar commitment since that time. With the increase in the power and speed of delivery of destruction that has come about over the last one-half century, it is increasingly necessary that the defenses of the Nation be in a ready condition at all times. We have repeatedly allowed them to deteriorate so that when the need arises we are unable to respond at the appropriate time and with the necessary strength. Most disappointing is the seeming lackadaisical attitude of much of the population in regard to really wanting to know the facts of the dangers that surround us at all times. Even more discouraging is the attitude that the "arm-chair" strategists are more capable of making the decisions that affect the safety and security of the Nation. They even arrive at the point of opposition to the actions that are required to maintain the safety of the citizens of this country. It is disappointing that the major news media of today does not report news but editorializes the news by the use of selective and biased reporting. A prime example is the reporting of the news from Iraq. The major media reports almost daily on the difficulties of building a new government, and on the attitudes of the people there. The service people when they write home and report to local news media have a story that is many times the absolute opposite of the news that has been reported to the Nation.

The foregoing statement prompts a series of "What If" questions. We can only appraise the actions that are taken—they are critiqued before, during and after they have been used. The options that are not used cannot be given the same level of scrutiny. The following is a list of What Ifs that a different option would have made for a different result.

1. What if—The Europeans had analyzed the dangers that were arising in the decade of the 30`s and taken action to counteract them earlier. Would the development of the war machines of Germany (Hitler) and Italy (Mussolini) have occurred, and would the other European Nations have been able to handle the problems that arose in the late 30`s and early 40`s?

2. What if—The world had recognized the danger of Japanese Imperialism (the war in China) during that same time frame and taken action to avoid the War in the Pacific that occurred in the 40`s. Would our country have been spared the brutal war in the Pacific if we had reacted earlier to the threat?

3. What if—The schools of our country had taught American and world history as it was, rather than embarking on an endeavor to frame history as a social study? Would a greater knowledge and appreciation of how our country was established, defended, and developed have created a higher level of patriotism during the time periods that we are referring to?

4. What if—The American citizens took the responsibilities of citizenship more seriously? Would we present a more united position to the threats to our Nation when they arise? Would we take our responsibilities of exercising our right to vote more seriously?

5. What if—We had recognized the danger of Communism in the late 40`s and realized that they were planning a world conquest. Could we have avoided the Korean War, the Vietnam War, and the Cold War?

6. What if—This Nation, the Free World, and the United Nations had been more effective in offsetting the advance of the Communist Agenda? Would the world's inhabitants be enjoying a more peaceful and prosperous life today and would they have enjoyed the same in the last one-half of the last century?

7. What if—The United Nations had been more effective in the cause of peace since its inception? It has proven many times over that it has little effect upon the tyrants of this time, and are of little value even as a debating society.

8. What if—The United Nations had been more effective in following the developing dangers of "genocide" in Africa and Asia? Would we have had to witness the problems in Rwanda, Bosnia, and the Middle East, and elsewhere? Would it have been possible to prevent the September 11, 2001 attack on the United States?

As the years have passed I have become much more aware of the impact that my experiences during this period of time has had on the rest of my life.

It has made me evaluate "Leadership" in a very different light. Some of what leadership requires was taught to me, some was learned by experience, but most of it was learned by observation. True leadership requires several things.

1. It requires a true commitment to the cause.
2. It requires a commitment to the needs of those that depend upon you for guidance and direction.
3. Never ask a subordinate to do anything that you would not do yourself.
4. It requires that you know what your assignment is, and the knowledge of how to carry it out effectively.
5. Be willing to "go the extra mile".
6. Success is accomplished by using all of the facilities that are available to you.
7. Always have a Plan B to use in the event that the first plan experiences difficulties.

I also learned that regardless of whether it is a military, civic, church, or business activity that needs leadership; the end results will show the quality of leadership by the level of success that is achieved. In short "the unit will show the quality of its leadership".

I also have come to realize that the real test of a person's character is determined by the beliefs and actions of the person. Ethnicity, nationality, race, or religion does not determine the quality of the person. I have come to realize that there are both "good" and "bad" in all of the foregoing categories. This was brought to my attention when my platoon contained a varied assortment of all of the categories, and we worked in harmony with each other. Even in the stressful event of the accidental shooting and death of one of the platoon members, there was no racial or ethnic repercussions of any kind. Also one of the Battalion Commanders (Major Kim) was a Korean that had been a victim of the concentration camp environment of the Japanese and Koreans by the Government of the U.S. in 1942. This in spite of the fact that they were United States citizens. He along with many others volunteered to serve in the military regardless of that treatment of their families. They served with distinction in Italy during that campaign and earned for themselves the honor and respect of the American people of that time. I knew him by sight and know that he achieved the rank of Colonel. He is now deceased. Colonel Wm. McCaffrey was our Regimental Commander when I arrived there and was immediately made aware of the honor and respect that the troops had for him. He earned it by his dedication to the cause and the desire for the best for those that served under him. He advanced to be a General before he retired from the Army. He also is now deceased. Another Regimental Commander that deserves mention is Colonel Moses, because he was also a very good leader, he was part Native-American and rose to the rank of General before he retired. He is also now deceased. I mention these as examples of the opportunities that are available to Americans of any and all descriptions if they have the character and desire to use their God-given talents.

As I review the material that is represented in this book, it becomes apparent that there is a need and a place for every serviceman or woman. They do not have to be in dangerous places to be of great value to the overall effort. The need for the logistical support of those troops is elementary in that the front-line troops cannot function without the support of those that serve behind them in many positions. An example of this is the situation that occurred in the spring of 1952. A dangerous condition was developing on the lines in Korea as the supply of munitions was not being delivered on time. The cause of the delay was a longshoreman's strike in San Francisco. President Truman resolved the issue by ordering the Army to load the ships. The troops were already on a daily ration of munitions. The final analysis is that the success of the mission is dependent upon many "LITTLE BITS" working as a team to accomplish the mission. I know that the success that I enjoyed requires recognition of the many that helped me to accomplish the mission that was assigned to me. I am grateful to all of them. It is my hope that the experience has made me a better man and citizen of this great Nation.

Even with all of the shortcomings and disappointments that the Democratic nations of this world have experienced, I am fully convinced that this form of government is the best that the human race has yet devised. I will close these remarks with a copy of an Armed Forces Talk on our own United States Democracy.

Extracts from Armed Forces Talk 212

Our Way of Life -- Democracy

We are a great people -- a great democracy. We have fought two World Wars on the side of Democracy. Our national policy has been to support democracy in all parts of the world.

What is democracy, our way of life?

Our democracy rests squarely on the Declaration of Independence. In the 52 words that make up the Preamble to the Constitution, our ideals of government have been expressed.

What do you think the framers of these documents had in mind? What did they mean "We, the People". The emphatic first place position of that phrase is significant. The delegates to the Constitutional Convention of 1787 gave top priority to the idea that the people themselves would establish their country's fundamental law and that the new government would be responsible to the people _____ not the other way around.

"Establish Justice". They wanted to make it clear that under the new government everyone would be entitled to and would get equal treatment under the laws, and in the courts. They wanted no more of the religious persecution, debtors' prisons, and indiscriminate property confiscation common in the 18th century Europe.

"Promote the General Welfare". The framers of the Constitution wanted it plainly understood that the Constitution would be concerned with the welfare of all, not the welfare of a priviledged few.

"And Secure the Blessings of Liberty to Ourselves and Our Posterity".

The delegates to the Constitutional Convention wanted to make absolutely certain that the new freedom, won by their country at great cost, would not be allowed to slip away.

These are some of the thoughts our forefathers must have had when they wrote the Declaration of Independence and the Preamble to the Constitution. Our goals for the future are the same -- liberty and justice for all, in a Union in which the people are supreme.

Almost as soon as the Constitution was adopted, 10 Amendments were added, known as the Bill of Rights, along with either sections of the Constitution they provided for freedom of religious belief, freedom of speech, of assembly, freedom from unreasonable search and seizure, the rights to petition, to keep and bear arms, and to trial by jury; The 13th 14th, and 15th amendments abolished all forms of slavery, gave citizenship to every person born or naturalized in the United States, and gave the rights to vote to all male citizens irrespective of race, color, or previous conditions of servitude. In 1920, the adoption of the 19th amendment gave women the right to vote.

(OVER)

Armed Forces Talk 212, page 1

Extracts from Armed Forces Talk 212 (Our Way of Life – Democracy) Cont'd

But Democracy means more than the words and provisions of the Constitution, the Bill of Rights, and any specific laws. Democracy is a system of human relations, a way in which people treat and deal with each other. As a system of human relations, democracy is based upon certain principles of action. The Golden Rule, "Do unto others as you would have them do unto you". Sums up these principles neatly. This principle of democratic pratice means more than treating the other fellow fairly and squarely. It means insisting that he gets his rights just as you get yours. You cannot give a single basic right or acquiese in the loss of a right by others, and expect to retain your own rights long.

Neither can you say that one right is more important than another. The interpendence of democratic rights is a important principle. Another principle of democratic action is that the majority rules but with due regard for minority opinion.

Democracy is based on certain faiths; The dignity and worth of the individual; the ability of man to govern themselves; the ability of men to learn. It is on the basis of these faiths that we believe in freedom, equality and our democratic institution.

One more important principle of democracy is that for every right there is always a corresponding duty. Among these duties are to respect the rights of others, to keep informed, to vote, to defend the country, and to be constructive by criticism.

Our democracy has been a successful democracy. The United States stands today as the freest of the nations and as the expression of the will of its people.

Our practice of democracy is faulty in some respects. We admit these faults. We tend, as time passes, to correct them. Our greatest danger however, lies in complacency. We cannot stop trying to improve our democracy, correct our undemocratic practices, and make our country more and more the "land of the free" that we proclaim it to be

Armed Forces Talk 212, page 2

It is hoped that this Nation will continue to build on the foundation that our Founders laid down for us over 230 years ago. Also that we will always remember that the words of President Lincoln—" A nation that is divided against itself cannot stand"—are as true today as when he spoke them almost 150 years ago.

I also realize that during my time in the army, the officers and men were not as reluctant to express their religious convictions as they seem to be today. I am fully convinced that the religious convictions of the men made them better soldiers and consequently more effective in carrying out their duties.